ANCIENT SYMBOL WORSHIP.

INFLUENCE OF THE PHALLIC IDEA

IN THE

RELIGIONS OF ANTIQUITY.

BY

HODDER M. WESTROPP

AND

C. STANILAND WAKE.

WITH AN

INTRODUCTION, ADDITIONAL NOTES, AND AN APPENDIX.

BY ALEXANDER WILDER, M.D.

SECOND EDITION, ILLUSTRATED.

NEW YORK:
J. W. BOUTON, 706 BROADWAY.
1875.

Entered according to Act of Congress, in the year 1874,
By JAMES W. BOUTON,
In the Office of the Librarian of Congress, at Washington.

Ancient Symbol Worship
ISBN 1-58509-048-4

© 1999
THE BOOK TREE
All Rights Reserved

Published by
The Book Tree
Post Office Box 724
Escondido, CA 92033

We provide controversial and educational products to help awaken the public to new ideas and information that would not be available otherwise. We carry over 1100 Books, Booklets, Audio, Video, and other products on Alchemy, Alternative Medicine, Ancient America, Ancient Astronauts, Ancient Civilizations, Ancient Mysteries, Ancient Religion and Worship, Angels, Anthropology, Anti-Gravity, Archaeology, Area 51, Assyria, Astrology, Atlantis, Babylonia, Townsend Brown, Christianity, Cold Fusion, Colloidal Silver, Comparative Religions, Crop Circles, The Dead Sea Scrolls, Early History, Electromagnetics, Electro-Gravity, Egypt, Electromagnetic Smog, Michael Faraday, Fatima, Fluoride, Free Energy, Freemasonry, Global Manipulation, The Gnostics, God, Gravity, The Great Pyramid, Gyroscopic Anti-Gravity, Healing Electromagnetics, Health Issues, Hinduism, Human Origins, Jehovah, Jesus, Jordan Maxwell, John Keely, Lemuria, Lost Cities, Lost Continents, Magic, Masonry, Mercury Poisoning, Metaphysics, Mythology, Occultism, Paganism, Pesticide Pollution, Personal Growth, The Philadelphia Experiment, Philosophy, Powerlines, Prophecy, Psychic Research, Pyramids, Rare Books, Religion, Religious Controversy, Roswell, Walter Russell, Scalar Waves, SDI, John Searle, Secret Societies, Sex Worship, Sitchin Studies, Smart Cards, Joseph Smith, Solar Power, Sovereignty, Space Travel, Spirituality, Stonehenge, Sumeria, Sun Myths, Symbolism, Tachyon Fields, Templars, Tesla, Theology, Time Travel, The Treasury, UFOs, Underground Bases, World Control, The World Grid, Zero Point Energy, and much more. Call **(800) 700-TREE** for our *FREE BOOK TREE CATALOG* or visit our website at www.thebooktree.com for more information.

Canesa,

THE GOD OF WISDOM, IN THE HINDU PANTHEON.

FOREWARD

Phallic worship has been practiced by many varied and widespread cultures throughout the world for thousands of years. The male phallic was recognized as the bringer of life and the progenitor of the human race. As with many ancient cultures, a more complete understanding of the phenomena of sexual intercourse was to remain a mystery and, even by today's standards, some of those mysteries remain.

It is evident that the belief of the reciprocal principles of nature, male and female, light and dark, active and passive; was known in most of the primitive religious systems of both the old and new worlds. Thus, what resulted was the widespread, common veneration paid to the sexual parts, as they were associated to the productive and generative principles in nature.

The origin of phallic worship is hidden behind so much obscurity that very little is actually known about it. The Phoenicians, Egyptians, Phrygians, Greeks, Hindus, and many others have legends and myths concerning phallic worship that date back to prehistory. This book explores the origins of phallic worship, its influence on the religions of antiquity, serpent symbolism, the tree of knowledge, the "fall of man," and sun-god worship in antiquity.

The intricate correlations that *Ancient Symbol Worship* makes concerning the origin of phallic worship throughout the world includes knowledge which is little known in today's world.

Tedd St. Rain

PREFACE.

THE historian Gibbon has remarked that "a lively desire of knowing and recording our ancestors so generally prevails, that it must depend on the influence of some common principle in the minds of men." To this we are probably to refer the inquisitiveness that leads individuals to the investigation of the relics of bygone periods, whether as naturalists, philologists, or historical inquirers. The Book of Genesis has been eagerly scrutinized as containing a divinely-inspired record of the Origin of Mankind; and ancient histories are carefully turned over in quest of clews in the same direction. The studies of language and etymology are interesting as affording traces of the ancestry of our modern peoples. The same plea holds good in regard to religious inquiry. Language and worship are crystallized history.

Unbecoming alike are the supercilious disdain and the sanctimonious contempt flung by pretentious men upon ancient ideas and usages. The ignorant cock that scorned the jewel because he knew not how to ascertain its value, and preferred the corn which he could scratch out from the dunghill, is an apt likeness of such persons. It is certainly proper to pay due regard to utility and present advantage. But the disposition to confine the attention to that limit is as imbruting and sensual as anything in fetish-worship or the orgies of the old-time divinities. The generous mind will cast aside such a temper, and, in obedience to its own instincts, hasten to broader fields of exploration, whether in natural science, metaphysical inquiry, or archæological investigation. Labor which makes a person better acquainted with himself or his fellow-men is not wasted.

In former periods it was the practice to check exuberant

curiosity by destroying records, and inflicting summary penalties on those who exceeded the bounds that had been set to scientific and literary pursuits. Cardinal Ximenes burned the old Arabic manuscripts; Galileo languished in prison; Socrates drank the hemlock, and Servetus perished at the stake; the Gauls destroyed the annals of Old Rome, and the Romans those of ancient Carthage and Spain; the Brahmins were alike malignant to the population and literature of Hindustan, and the Moslems equally destructive to the books that fell in their way from Benares and Bactria to Syria and Alexandria. All hoped in this way to put an end to the supremacy of scholars and rival nations, and to confine thought to the metes and limits of religious orthodoxy. They succeeded for a time, but only partially. Knowledge extinguished in one place broke forth in another; and every nation that burned records and slaughtered teachers speedily declined into insignificance. At the present time the *Index Expurgatorius* of the Vatican, so far from excluding books from general reading, has become the best medium for advertising them; and the achievements of Omar at Alexandria, Nabonasar at Babylon, and Torquemeda at Salamanca, to be successful, would require a general holocaust. Those who protest against scientific and archæological studies as tending to unsettle the mind in regard to accepted doctrines, are speaking too late. Devotion which is born of ignorance is not worthy of being cherished.

Nevertheless, there is little ground for apprehension that the foundations of a genuine religious belief will be undermined. The investigation of the beginnings of a religion is never the work of infidels, but of the most reverent and conscientious minds. Those who are at liberty to develop themselves freely, will seldom molest themselves about the opinions of others. Mystics and philosophers do not clash, but often arrive at like conclusions by different routes and the exercise of different faculties of mind.

The papers of Messrs. Westropp and Wake, showing the influence of "phallism" upon former religious ideas, are entitled to a candid and careful perusal. The ripe scholarship of those gentlemen is beyond question; and the fidelity with which they performed their labor is worthy of praise. They have treated the subject with a delicacy that is commendable, and with a dignity and fairness characteristic of the scholar and the sage. Their purpose, as will be perceived, is not merely to portray its features, but to exhibit it in its relations to modern idea.

This much is claimed especially for the investigations noted in these pages. Whatever may be thought of the men who, according to our modern notions, took such extraordinary views of divine things and resorted to what would be regarded as offensive methods to express them, it is certain nevertheless that in important respects they were equal, if not superior, to the foremost thinkers of our boasted nineteenth century. Our architects learned of them how to build; and they possessed accurate scientific knowledge. Our theories of government, modes of inquiry, and even our religious opinions, were derived from the same sources. If we have degraded the ideas which they cherished with reverence, if we have rendered obscene the mysteries of life which they adored as pure and instituted by God himself, let us not add to the injury by endeavoring to cast upon them the reproach which belongs to those who thus calumniate them.

Herein, it may be, the ancients have us at disadvantage. They worshipped the Supreme Being as the Father of men, and saw no impurity in the symbolism of parentage to indicate the work of creation. What is divine to be and to do cannot be immodest and wicked to express. No man born of woman can with decency impugn the operation of that law to which he owes his existence; and he is impious beyond others who regards that law as only sensual. We may easily perceive how the phallic emblems were adopted to denote the kinship of mankind to the Creator. Those who employed them apprehended no wrong in so doing, till impurity of life had caused all that related to the subject to be considered as indecorous.

In these pages the endeavor has been to discourse of the several topics without levity or discourtesy toward any individual or people. There may be views taken which differ essentially from those commonly entertained, but there is no design to treat any person, topic, or opinion with disrespect. It will also be seen, from the references, that the facts here presented have generally been long familiar to the educated public. The subject is interesting, not merely because of its peculiar character, but as affording more complete views of ethnology, as well as of the earlier development of religious thought. Nothing of value can be lost, and much will be gained in every way, by investigation pursued with candor and dispassionately.

INTRODUCTION.

> BAAL. . . . . None older is than I. When Man came forth,
> The final effort, wrung from monstrous forms,
> And Earth's outwearied forces could no more,
> I warmed the ignorant bantling on my breast.
> We rose together, and my kingdom spread
> From these cold hills to hamlets in the palms,
> That grew to Memphis and to Babylon :
> While I on towers and hanging terraces,
> In shaft and obelisk, beheld my sign
> Creative, shape of first imperious law.
> "*Masque of the Gods*," by BAYARD TAYLOR.

THE classic scholar whose studies have hardly exceeded the limits prescribed in the curriculum of the universities, and the biblical student whose explorations of the Hebrew Scriptures have not led him beyond the field of exegesis and theological pursuit, are ill-prepared to hear of a larger world than Greece, Rome, and Palestine, or of an archaic time which almost remands the annals of those countries into the domain of modern history. Olympian Zeus with his college of associate deities, afterward Latinized into Jupiter and his divine subordinates, and the Lord alone with his ten thousands of sacred ones, comprise their idea of the supernal world and its divinities. Beyond, they recognize a vague and misty chaos of mythologies, which, not accurately understanding, they superciliously affect to despise. Whoever would be really intelligent, must boldly explore that chaos, voyaging through the "outer world" away from Troy and Greece, as far as Ulysses went, and from biblical scenes to the very heart of the ancient empires. There is no occasion for terror, like that displayed by the mariners who sailed with Columbus into the unknown ocean. Wherever man is to be found, like instincts, passions, hopes, and ambitions will attest a common kindred. Each person's life is in some manner repeated in that of his fellows, and every human soul is a mirror in which other souls, as well as future and former events, reflect their image.

It is more than probable that the diversified customs, institutions, and religions of the several nations of the world are less dissimilar in their origin than is often imagined. The differences uprose in the progress of time, the shifting scenes of climate, condition, and event. But the original ideas of existence, and the laws which pertain to all created things, are pretty much the same among the various tribes of mankind. The religions, philosophical systems and symbolisms, are outgrowths,—the aspirations of thinking and reverential men to solve and express in suitable form the facts which underlie and constitute all things.

We should therefore approach the subject of human faith and worship with candor, modesty, and respect. Men's beliefs are entitled to so much. The unwitting individual may be astonished at beholding men, the masters of the science and thought of their time, adoring gods that are represented as drunken and adulterous, and admitting extravagant stories and scandalous narrations among their religious verities. In his simplicity he may conceive that he has a right to contemn, and even to scoff at, such prodigious infatuation. But the infatuation and absurdity are only apparent. There is a fuller, profounder meaning, which sanctifies the emblems and legends which ignorant and superficial men denounce. M. Rénan speaks justly as well as eloquently: "It is sacrilege, in a religious light, this making sport of symbols consecrated by Time, wherein, too, man had deposited his first views of the divine world." *

Religions were never cunningly devised by priests, or ambitious leaders, for the purpose of enabling them to hold the human mind in abject bondage. Nor did they come into existence, full-grown, like Athené, the Jove-born; nor were they constructed from the lessons of sages or even of prophets. They were born, like men, not mature but infantile; the body and life as a single entity, without a definite evolving of the interior, symbolized idea, yet containing all potentially; so that time and growth were required to enable the intelligent mind to distinguish rightly between the form and the substance which it envelops and shadows forth. When this substance, like the human soul, has fully developed, the external forms and symbols become of little value, and are cast off and rejected like chaff from the wheat. Yet for the sake of their use they are to be valued and respected. The well-thinking medical student never indulges in ribald hilarity at or in the presence of the corpse which he dissects, from reverence for

* *Études d'Histoire Religieuse*, Frothingham's translation.

the human soul that was once its tenant. But religious symbols lose their sacredness when they are employed to supplant the idea which alone had rendered them valuable.

Let there be no contempt, then, for the Children of the Mist, who love to gaze backward into the past to ascertain what man has been, and to look within to learn what he is and ought to be. They are not prophets without inspiration, or apostles that have no mission. Behind the vail is the Shekinah; only the anointed have authority to lift aside the curtain.

Modern science somewhat audaciously has endeavored to set aside the time-honored traditions of a Golden Age. We do not undertake to controvert the new doctrine, so necessary to establish the recently-traced relationships between men and monkeys. The same social law which allows every man to choose his own company, can be extended perhaps to the selection of his kindred.

But, so far as we are able to perceive, there have been cycles of human development, analogous to the geological periods, that have been accomplished upon the earth. Men, nations, and civilizations, like the seasons, have passed over the great theatre of existence. We have often only the traces of them in a few remains of language, manufacture, and religion. Much is lost save to conjecture. Judging from our later observations of human progress, there must have been a long term of discipline that schooled them; yet, perhaps, it was the divine intuition and instinct implanted in them that enabled them to achieve so much. It is not possible, however, to extend researches back far enough to ascertain. We are not equal to the task of describing the fossils of a perished world. We are compelled to read the archaic history through the forms and mysteries * of

---

* By *mysteries* the educated reader will not understand merely doctrines or symbols, or even secrets as such, but a system of discipline and instruction in esoteric learning which was deemed too sacred and recondite for those who had not complied with the essential conditions. Every ancient country had its sacerdotal order, the members of which had been initiated into the mysteries; and even Jesus defended his practice of discoursing in parables or allegories, because that only to his disciples was it given to understand the mysteries of the kingdom of God, whereas to the multitude it was not given. The priests of Egypt, the Magians of the ancient countries beyond the river Euphrates, the priests of Phœnicia and the other countries of Western Asia, were all members of sacerdotal colleges that might not divulge the esoteric knowledge to the uninitiated. Even the Brahmins of India are said

religion, and the peculiarities of language, rather than in the pages of the annalist. The amber of mythology has served to preserve to us the most of what is to be learned on these topics.

The primitive religion of mankind is perhaps only to be ascertained when we know accurately their original habitats. But this, like the gilded butterfly, eludes our search. India, Persia, Babylonia, Syria, Phœnicia, Egypt, were but colonies. The Vendidad indicates a country north of the river Oxus; and Sir William Jones, adopting the story of the learned Sufi, Mohsan Fani, declared his belief that a powerful monarchy once existed there long before the Assyrian empire; the history of which was engrafted upon that of the Hindoos, who colonized the country between the river Indus and the Bay of Bengal. In conformity with the views of this writer, Sir William accordingly describes the primeval religion of Iran and the Aryan peoples as consisting of "a firm belief that One Supreme God made the world by his power and continually governed it by his providence:—a pious fear, love, and adoration of him;—a due reverence for parents and aged persons; a paternal affection for the whole human species, and a compassionate tenderness even for the brute creation."

But, however much of truth there may be in this description, it evidently relates only to the blonde races. We see plainly enough the engrafting of "history," or rather legends, in many other countries, as well as among the Brahmins of India. The Hebrew records, tracing their patriarchs to Egypt and Assyria, are prob-

---

to have also their mysteries at the present time; and the late Godfrey Higgins relates that a Mr. Ellis was enabled, by aid of the masonic tokens, to enter the penetralia of a temple in the presidency of Madras. That there is some such "freemasonry" existing in many of the countries which we denominate uncivilized and pagan, is probable. The early Christians and heretical sects had also their signs of recognition, and were distinguished like the initiates of the older worships, according to their grade, as *neophytes* (1 Timothy iii. 6), *spiritual*, and *perfect*. The mysteries most familiar to classical readers are the Eleusinia, which appear to have descended from the prehistoric periods. Pococke declares them to have been of Tartar origin, which is certainly plausible, and to have combined Brahminical and Buddhistical ideas. Those admitted only to the Lesser Mysteries were denominated *Mystæ*, or *vailed;* those initiated into the Greater Mysteries were *epoptai*, or seers. Socrates was not initiated, yet after drinking the hemlock he addresses Crito: "We owe a cock to Æsculapius." This was the peculiar offering made by initiates on the eve of the last day, and he thus sublimely asserted that he was about to receive the great apocalypse.

ably no exception. The Garden of Eden appears to have been well known to the king of Tyre (Ezekiel xxviii. 13–16), who is styled "the anointed cherub;" the Assyrian is also described (xxxi. 3–18) as a cedar in Lebanon, "fair by the multitude of his branches, so that all the trees of Eden that were in the garden of God envied him;" and Pharaoh, king of Egypt, is also assured that he shall "be brought down with the trees of Eden into the nether parts of the earth." From that region Abraham is reputed to have emigrated, and its traditions are probably therefore consecrated as religious legends.

If we had time and space to follow this subject, we might be able to show that the period when the Hebrew patriarch is supposed to have removed from the region of the Upper Euphrates, revolutions were occurring there which changed the structure of society. "Your fathers," said Joshua to the assembled Israelites, "your fathers dwelt on the other side of the flood in old time, even Terah, the father of Abraham and the father of Nahor; and they served other gods." * The Persian legend of "Airyana-vaeja, of the good creation which Anra-mainyas (Ahriman) full of death filled with evils," † and the Hebrew story of the garden of Eden ‡ which was by the headwaters of the Oxus, Tigris, and Euphrates, where dwelt the man and the woman till the successful invasion of the Serpent, indicate the Great Religious War of which traditions exist in the principal countries of ancient time. It occurred between the nations of the East and the nations of the West, the Iranians and Turanians, the Solar and Lunar nations, the Lingacitas and the Yonijas, those who venerated images and religious symbols, and those who discarded them. Vast bodies of men were compelled to abandon their homes, many of them skilled in the arts of civilization and war. Tribes and dynasties emigrated to escape slavery and destruction; and other climates received and cherished those who had been deemed unworthy to live. These events are superimposed upon the history of every people. Whether the migration mentioned by Juno of the *gens inimica*, the Trojans, from Troy to Italy, bearing its political genius and conquered divinities, depicts any actual occurrence, we do not undertake to say; but convulsions did take place, by which peoples once living as one nation, the Hindoos and Persians, Greeks and Romans, Germans and Slaves, were divided

* Joshua xxiv. 2.   † *Vendidad*, i. 5–12.   ‡ Genesis ii. and iii.

from each other and removed to other regions. The Ethiopian or Hamitic races underwent a like overturning and dispersion, probably from their contests with the blonde invaders of the North. Thus, the second chapter of Genesis describes the river Pison, as compassing the land of Ethiopia or Cush, which was evidently situated upon the Erythræan or Arabian Sea. The people of this region appear to have occupied or colonized India, Babylonia, Arabia, Syria, Egypt, and other countries of the West. They were the builder-race *par excellence;* and carried civilization, architecture, mathematical science, their arts and political institutions wherever they went. Their artisans, doubtless, erected the temples and pyramids of Egypt, India, and Babylon; excavated the mountain of Ellora, the islands of Salsette and Elephanta, the artificial caves of Bamian, the rocks of Petra and the hypogea of Egypt; built the houses of Ad in Arabia, the Cyclopean structures of India, Arabia, and the more western countries; constructed ships for the navigation of the seas and oceans, and devised the art of sculpture. Mathematics and astronomy, alphabetical as well as hieroglyphical writing, and many other sciences, perhaps those which have been *discovered* in later times, were possessed and cultivated by these "blameless Æthiopians,* most ancient of men."

The Hebrew Scriptures, which have been regarded as especially the oracles of religious truth, develop the fact, as has been already suggested, of a close resemblance of the earlier Israelites with the surrounding nations. Their great progenitor, Abraham, is described as emigrating from the region of Chaldea, at the junction of the Tigris and Euphrates, in the character of a dissenter from the religion of that country.† Yet he and his imme-

---

* The term *Æthiopian* cannot be regarded, when applied to any ancient people, as indicating negro or negroid origin. Like other names, it had a religious meaning, and was applied to Zeus or Jupiter, and also to Prometheus. The best-defined opinion connects it with the serpent-worship, which prevailed, along with that of the lingam, among the Cushite and kindred peoples. It is noticeable that ethnology has given the Chinese and Mongolian tribes a world apart. There seems to be a wall between them and the populations of other climates. The Chinese nevertheless manifested themselves occasionally upon the surface of Asiatic history; and the Tartars have often appeared as invaders and conquerors, designated in the metaphors and allegories of the old languages, as floods of waters, destroying the world.

† Joshua xxiv. 2, 3.

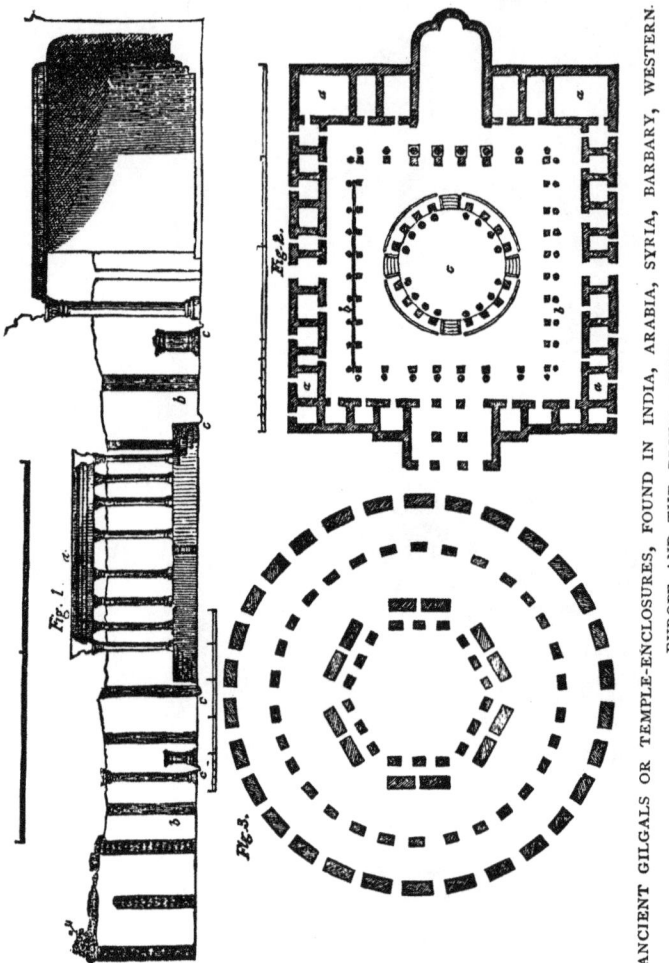

ANCIENT GILGALS OR TEMPLE-ENCLOSURES, FOUND IN INDIA, ARABIA, SYRIA, BARBARY, WESTERN EUROPE AND THE BRITISH ISLES.

Introduction.

diate descendants appear to have at least employed the same religious symbols and forms of worship as the people of Canaan and Phœnicia, who are recorded to have already occupied Palestine.* He erected altars wherever he made a residence; and "planted a grove" or pillar in Beer-sheba, as a religious emblem.† He is also represented as conducting his son to the land of Moriah, to immolate him as a sacrifice to the Deity, as was sometimes done by the Phœnicians; and as was afterwards authorized in the Mosaic law.‡ One of the *suffets*, or judges, Jephthah the Gileadite, in like manner sacrificed his own daughter at Mizpeh; § and the place where Abraham built his altar was afterwards selected as the site for the temple of Solomon.‖ Jacob is twice mentioned as setting up a pillar, calling the place Beth-el,¶ and as making libations. On the occasion also of forming a treaty of amity with his father-in-law, Laban, the Syrian, he erected a pillar and directed his brethren to pile up a cairn, or heap of stones; to which were applied the names Galeed, or circle, and Mizpeh, or pillar. Monoliths, or "great stones," appear to have been as common in Palestine as in other countries, and the cairns and circles (gilgals) were equally so, as well as the mounds or "high places." The *suffets*,** or "judges," and the kings, maintained them till Hezekiah. Samuel the prophet worshipped at a high place at Ramah, and Solomon at the "great stone," or high place in Gibeon.†† There were also priests,‡‡ and we suspect *kadeshim*, stationed at them. At Mizpeh, probably at the pillar, was a seat of government of the Israelites; and Joshua set up a pillar under the oak of Shechem, by the sanctuary. Jephthah the judge made his residence at the former place, and his daugh-

---

* Genesis xii. 6; xiii. 7.
† Genesis xxi. 33.
‡ Leviticus xxvii. 28, 29.
§ Judges xi. 30, 31, and 34–40.
‖ 2 Chronicles iii. 1.
¶ Genesis xxxviii. 18–22; xxxv. 1–15.
** The suffet was a magistrate under the *Phœnician* system, as is observed at Carthage. The patriarchal government was that of *sheiks*, as among the nomadic Arabs, while the Israelites of Goshen and the desert are described as being organized like the Arabs of the towns.
†† 1 Kings iii. 4. See also ch. xv. 14; xv. 14; xv. 14; xxii. 43. 2 Kings xii. 2; xiv. 4; xv. 4.
‡‡ 2 Kings xxiii. 9.

ter, the Iphigenia of the Book of Judges, was immolated there. Samuel was also inaugurated there as *suffet* of Israel. There were other "great stones" mentioned, as Abel, Bethshemesh or Heliopolis; Ezel, where David met with Jonathan; and Ebenezer, erected by Samuel on the occasion of a victory over the Philistines.

But Hezekiah appears to have changed the entire Hebrew religious polity. He removed the Hermaic or Dionysiac statues, and the conical omphalic emblems of Venus-Ashtoreth; overthrew the mounds and altars, and broke in pieces the serpent of brass made by Moses, to which the people had burned incense "unto those days." Josiah afterwards also promulgated the law of Moses, and was equally iconoclastic. He removed the paraphernalia of the worship of the sun, destroyed the image of Semel, or Hermes, expelled the *kadeshim*, or consecrated men and women, from the cloisters of the Temple, and destroyed the statutes and emblems of Venus and Adonis. *

We have suggested that Abraham was represented in the character of a dissenter from the worship prevailing at "Ur of the Khasdim." As remarked on a subsequent page by Mr. Wake, "that some great *religious* movement, ascribed by tradition to Abraham, did take place among the Semites at an early date, is undoubted." It may have been the "Great Religious War." The religion of the patriarchs appears to have had some affinity with that of the Persians, insomuch that some writers intimate an identity of origin. This was certainly the case at a later period. Other peoples were also driven to emigration. Many Scythian nations abandoned their former seats. The Phœnicians left their country on the Erythrean Sea, and emigrated to the shores of the Mediterranean. The Pali, or shepherds on the Indus, removed to the west. A part of the population of Asiatic Ethiopia, or Beluchistan, it is supposed, also emigrated. The Hyk-sos,† during the Sixth Dynasty of the Old Monarchy,

---

* 2 Kings xxiii. 4–20.

† Manetho translates this term, from the "sacred language," kingly shepherds; *hyk* signifying king, and *sos* a shepherd. He seems to hesitate, however, for he also remarks that "some say that they were Arabians," and that "in the sacred books they were also styled captives." *Shos* signifies Arabian, and *sus* a horse. Are we not allowed to suppose them to be *shepherds* as rearing and using horses? They appear to have introduced the horse into Egypt, which makes this idea seem plausible.

Introduction. 17

appeared in Egypt. Josephus, abandoning his own history of Jewish Antiquities, construes the account by Manetho, in regard to them, as relating to the ancient Hebrews, remarking: "Our ancestors had the dominion over their country." * If we might interpret the story of Abraham and other patriarchs as we would the traditions of other nations, we would assign to it a religious or esoteric meaning rather than a secular and historical one, and fix a later period for the beginning of the authentic annals. The early association of the Shemitic with the Ethiopian nations, however, appears to be abundantly corroborated by profane as well as sacred history.

Similarity of customs indicate that the "chosen people," if they had a separate political existence, were in other respects substantially like the earlier nations. We may expect to find these resemblances close enough to show even a family likeness. Of course, every intelligent reader is aware that the Hamitic and Shemitic populations of Asia, Africa, and Europe, belonged to what is denominated the Caucasian or Indo-Germanic race.

The earliest deity of the Ethiopian or Hamitic nations, whose worship was most general, was the one known in the Bible by the designation of Baal. He bore, of course, a multiplicity of titles, which were often personified as distinct אלהים *aleim*, or divinities; besides having in Syria a separate name for every season of the year. In the Sanscrit language he was styled *Maha Deva*, or Supreme God; and after the Aryan conquest, was added to the Brahmin Trimourti under the title Siva. Other names are easily traced in the Hamitic languages; as Bala in Bel, the tutelar deity of Babylon; Deva Nahusha, or Dionysus, of Arabia and Thrace; Iswara, or Oseiris, of Egypt. In western mythology he become more generally known through the Phœnicians. In Tyre he was Mel-karth, the lord of the city; in Syria he was Adonis and Moloch; but all through Europe he is best known by the hero-name Hercules. His twelve labors typify the sun passing through the signs of the zodiac; his conquests in the west show whither the Phœnician navigators directed their course; while the maypoles, Bâl-fires, and other remnants of old worships, exist as his memorials. The story of his achievements is a fair outline of the history of Phœnician adventure.

* *Against Apion*, i. 25.

Introduction.

"The wonderful and universal power of light and heat," says that most modest and amiable writer, Mrs. Lydia Maria Child,* "has caused the Sun to be worshipped as a visible emblem of deity in the infancy of nearly all nations. Water is recognized as another obvious symbol of divine influence. Hence the sacred rivers, fountains, and wells abounding in Hindostan. The Air is likewise to them a consecrated emblem. Invisible, pervading all space, and necessary to the life of all creatures, it naturally suggests the spirit of God. Nearly all languages describe the soul by some phrase similar in signification to 'the *breath* of life.' Brahm is sometimes called Alma, or the Breathing Soul.

"Other emblems deemed sacred by the Hindoos, and worshipped in their temples, have brought upon them the charge of gross indecency. But if it be true at the present time, it probably was not so at the beginning. When the world was in its infancy, people spoke and acted with more of the simplicity and directness of little children than they do at present. In the individual child, and in the childhood of society, whatever is incomprehensible produces religious awe. As the reflective faculties develop, man is solemnly impressed with the wonders of creation, in the midst of which his soul wakes up, as it were, from a dream. And what so miraculous as the advent of this conscious soul into the marvellous mechanism of a human body? If Light with its grand revealings, and Heat making the earth fruitful with beauty, excited wonder and worship in the first inhabitants of our world, is it strange that they likewise regarded with reverence the great mystery of human Birth? Were *they* impure thus to regard it? Or, are we impure that we do *not* so regard it? We have travelled far, and unclean have been the paths, since those old anchorites first spoke of God and the soul in the solemn depths of their first sanctuaries. Let us not smile at their mode of tracing the Infinite and Incomprehensible Cause throughout all the mysteries of Nature, lest by so doing we cast the shadow of our own grossness on their patriarchal simplicity.

"From time immemorial, an emblem has been worshipped in Hindostan as the type of creation,† or the origin of life. It

---

* *Progress of Religious Ideas through Successive Ages.* Vol. 1, pp. 15, 16, 17.

† The first verse of the Book of Genesis declares creation to have been a

AN ENTABLATURE REPRESENTING THE SAKTI PUJA, OR WORSHIP OF THE LINGA-YONI IN INDIA.

is the most common symbol of Siva [Baal or Maha Deva], and is universally connected with his worship. To understand the original intention of this custom, we should remember that Siva was not merely the reproducer of human forms; he represented the Fructifying Principle, the Generating Power that pervades the universe, producing sun, moon, stars, men, animals, and plants. The symbol to which we have alluded is always in his temples. It is usually placed in the inmost recess, or sanctuary, sculptured in granite, marble, or ivory, often crowned with flowers, and surmounted by a golden star. Lamps are kept burning before it, and on festival occasions it is illuminated by a lamp with seven branches, supposed to represent the planets.* Small images of this emblem, carved in ivory, gold, or crystal, are often worn as ornaments about the neck. The pious use them in their prayers, and often have them buried with them. Devotees of Siva have it written on their foreheads in the form of a perpendicular mark. The maternal emblem is likewise a religious type; and worshippers of Vishnu represent it on their forehead by a horizontal mark, with three short perpendicular lines."

These symbols are found in the temple-excavations of the islands of Salsette and Elephanta, of unknown antiquity; in the grotto-temples of Ellora, at the "Seven Pagodas." on the Coromandel coast, in the old temple at Tanjore, and elsewhere, where Siva-worship is in the ascendant. Although these symbols, the lingam and yoni, have been adopted by the Brahmins, there is little harmony between the Lingayats and Vishnavites. " In the sacrifice of Wisdom," says Daksha, "no Brahmin is wanted to officiate." The Rig-Veda denounces the "lascivious wretches" who adore the sexual emblems, in such language as this: "Let not the lascivious wretches approach our sacred rites. †
"The irresistible [Indra] overcame the lascivious wretches."

In her chapter on Egypt, Mrs. Child again remarks : " Because plants cannot germinate without water, vases full of it were

series of *Toledoth*, or generations. It is properly translated: "God (the *Aleim*) engendered (B'RA) the heavens and the earth."

* The seven-branched candlestick of the Mosaic tabernacle has here its prototype.

† *Rig-Veda*, vii. 21 : 5; and x. 99 : 3. The term used is *Sisna-devas*, or phallus-gods.

carried at the head of processions in honor of Oseiris, and his votaries refrained from destroying or polluting any spring. This reverence for the production of Life, introduced into his worship the sexual emblems so common in Hindostan. A colossal image of this kind was presented to his temple in Alexandria, by King Ptolemy Philadelphus. Crowned with gold and surmounted by a golden star, it was carried in a splendid chariot in the midst of religious processions. A serpent, the emblem of Immortality, always accompanies the image of Oseiris." . . .

"Reverence for the mystery of organized life led to the recognition of a masculine and feminine principle in all things spiritual or material. Every elemental force was divided into two, the parents of other forces. The active wind was masculine, the passive mist, or inert atmosphere, was feminine. Rocks were masculine, the productive earth was feminine. The presiding deity of every district [*nome*] was represented as a Triad or Trinity. At Thebes it was Amun, the creative Wisdom; Neith, the spiritual Mother; and a third, supposed to represent the Universe. At Philæ it was Oseiris, the generating Cause; Isis, the receptive Mould, and Horus, the Result. The sexual emblems everywhere conspicuous in the sculptures of their temples would seem impure in description, but no clean and thoughtful mind could so regard them while witnessing the obvious simplicity and solemnity with which the subject is treated."

"All the idolaters of that day," says Colonel Tod,* seem to have held the grosser tenets of Hinduism. . . When Judah did evil in the sight of the Lord, and 'built them high places and images and groves [mounds, hermaic pillars, and omphalic statues] on every high hill and under every green tree,' the object was Bál; and the pillar (the lingam, matzebah or phallus) was his symbol.† It was on his altar that they burned incense, and 'sacrificed unto the Calf on the fifteenth day of the eighth month,' the sacred Amavus of the Hindus. The Calf of Israel is the Bull (nanda) of Bálcesar or Iswara, the Apis of the Egyptian Oseiris. . . Mahadeva, or Iswara, is the tutelary divinity of the Rajpoots in Mewar, and from the early annals of the dynasty appears to have been, with his consort Isa, the sole object of

---

* *Rajasthan*, vol. i., 76-79.
† 1 Kings xiv. 22. The introduction of *kadeshim*, or persons consecrated and set apart, like nautch-girls, or *almas*, is first mentioned in this connection.

Gehlote adoration. Iswara is adored under the epithet of Eklinga, and is either worshipped in his monolithic symbol, or as Iswara Chaomukhi, the quadriform divinity represented by a bust with four faces."

These spectacles, however, were regarded as sacred, and few regarded them as possessing moral turpitude. "This worship was so general as to have spread itself over a large part of the habitable globe; for it flourished for many ages in Egypt and Syria, Persia, Asia Minor, Greece, and Italy; it was and still is in vigor in India and many parts of Africa, and was even found in America on its discovery by the Spaniards." *

Being regarded as the most sacred objects of worship, and consecrated by religion, the cultus was associated with every idea and sentiment which was regarded as ennobling to man. The reflecting men of all the older ages, down to Plato, Plotinus, Iamblichus, and the followers of the Gnosis, all paid like respect to the great arcanum of life and of Man. We need not look superciliously upon their veneration; for however different our modes of thought, however exaggerated above theirs our fastidiousness, we cannot escape the same problems which they thus labored to solve, nor the necessity to realize the vailing and the apocalypse which the symbols and the mysteries foreshadowed.

* *Aphrodisiacs and Anti-Aphrodisiacs.* Three Essays on the Powers of Reproduction, with some Account of the Judicial "Congress," as practised in France during the Seventeenth Century. By John Davenport. Small quarto, with eight full-page illustrations. London, 1869.

PHALLIC WORSHIP.*

BY HODDER M. WESTROPP.

HUMAN NATURE is the same in all climes; and the workings of this same human nature are almost identical in the different stages of its growth. Hence similar and analogous ideas, beliefs, and superstitious practices are frequently evolved independently among different peoples. These are the result of suggestions arising spontaneously in the human mind at certain stages of its development, and which seem almost universal.

As a remarkable instance of this, I have drawn up the following sketch of phallic worship, which was one of those beliefs or superstitious practices which have sprung up independently, and which seem to have extensively prevailed among many nations.

It will acquire additional interest when it is considered that it is the most ancient of the superstitions of the human race, that it has prevailed more or less among all known people in ancient times, and that it has been handed down even to a very late and Christian period.

In the earlier ages the operations of nature made a stronger impression on the minds of men. Those ideas, springing from the constant observation of the modes of acting in nature, were consequently more readily suggested to the minds of all races of men in the primitive ages.

Two causes must have forcibly struck the minds of men in those early periods when observant of the operations of nature, one the generative power, and the other the productive, the active and passive causes. This double mode

* A paper read before the Anthropological Society of London, April 5th, 1870.

of production visible in nature must have given rise to comparisons with the mode of proceeding in the generation of animals, in which two causes concur, the one active and the other passive, the one male and the other female, the one as father, the other as mother. These ideas were doubtless suggested independently and spontaneously in different countries ; for the human mind is so constituted that the same objects and the same operations of nature will suggest like ideas in the minds of men of all races, however widely apart.

Nature to the early man was not brute matter, but a being invested with his own personality, and endowed with the same feelings, passions, and performing the same actions. He could only conceive the course of nature from the analogy to his own actions. Generation, begetting—production, bringing forth—were thus his ideas of cause and effect. The earth was looked upon as the mould of nature, as the recipient of seeds, the nurse of what was produced in its bosom ; the sky was the fecundating and fertilizing power. An analogy was suggested in the union of the male and female. These comparisons are found in ancient writers. " The sky," Plutarch says, "appeared to men to perform the functions of a father, as the earth those of a mother. The sky was the father, for it cast seed into the bosom of the earth, which in receiving them became fruitful and brought forth, and was the mother."

This union has been sung in the following verses by Virgil :

> " Tum pater omnipotens fecundis imbribis æther
> Conjugis in gremium lætæ descendit."—*Geor.* II.

Columella has related, in his treatise on agriculture, the loves of nature, or the marriage of heaven and earth, which takes place in the spring of the year.

These ideas bear a prominent part in the religious creeds of several nations. In Egypt the Deity or principle of generation was Khem, called " the father "—the abstract idea of father ; as the goddess Maut was that of mother. The office of Khem was not confined to the procreation and continuation of the human species, but extended even to the vegetable world, over which he presided, when we find his statue accompanied by trees and plants; and kings offering to him herbs of the ground, cutting the corn before him, or employed in his presence tilling the land, and preparing it to receive the generating influence of the deity.

In the Saiva Purana of the Hindoos, Siva says: "From the supreme spirit proceed Purusha (the generative or male principle), Prakriti (the productive or female principle), and Tirue; and by them was produced this universe, the manifestation of the one god. . . . Of all organs of sense and intellect, the best is mind, which proceeds from Ahankara, Ahankara from intellect, intellect from the supreme being, who is, in fact, Purusha. It is the primeval male, whose form constitutes the universe, and whose breath is the sky; and though incorporeal, that male am I." In the Kritya Tatwa, Siva is thus addressed by Brahma: "I know that Thou, O Lord, art the eternal Brahm, that seed which, being received in the womb of thy Sakti (aptitude to conceive), produced this universe; that thou united with thy Sakti dost create the universe from thine own substance like the web from the spider." In the same creed Siva is the personification of the sun (which he is equally with Surya) or fire, the genial heat which pervades, generates and vivifies all; and Bhavani, who, as the goddess of nature is also the earth, is the universal mother.

Among the Assyrians, the supreme god, Bel, was styled "the procreator"; and his wife, the goddess Mylitta, represented the productive principle of nature, and received the title of the queen of fertility. Another deity, the god Vul, the god of the atmosphere, is styled the beneficent chief, the giver of abundance, the lord of fecundity. On Assyrian cylinders he is represented as a phallic deity. With him is associated a goddess Shala, whose ordinary title is "Sarrat," queen, the feminine of the word "Sar," which means chief. Sir Henry Rawlinson remarks, with regard to the Assyrian San, or Shamas, the sun-god, that the idea of the motive influence of the sun-god in all human affairs arose from the manifest agency of the material sun in stimulating the functions of nature. In Phœnician mythology, Ouranos (heaven) weds Ghè (the earth), and by her becomes father of Oceanus, Hyperon, Iapetus, Cronos, and other gods. In conformity with the religious ideas of the Greeks and Romans, Virgil describes the products of the earth as the result of the conjugal act between Jupiter (the sky) and Juno (the earth). According to St. Augustin, the sexual organ of man was consecrated in the temple of Liber, that of woman in the sanctuaries of Libera; these two divinities were named father and mother.

In the month of April, when the fertilizing powers of nature begin to operate and its productive powers to be visibly developed, a festival in honor of Venus took place at Rome; in it the phallus was carried in a cart, and led in procession by the Roman ladies to the temple of Venus outside the Colline gate, and then presented by them to the sexual parts of the goddess. This is only symbolizing the same idea as expressed by Virgil in the *Georgics*. We find similar ideas in the religious creeds of America, and of the remote islands of the Pacific Ocean. According to the Indians of Central America, Famagostad and Zipaltonal, the first male and the second female, created heaven, earth, man, and all things.

The Tahitians imagined that everything which exists in the universe proceeds from the union of two beings: one of them was named Taroataihetounou; the other Tepapa: they were supposed to produce continually and by connection the days and months. Those islanders supposed that the sun and moon, which are gods, had begotten the stars, and that the eclipses were the time of their copulation.

A New Zealand myth says we have two primeval ancestors, a father and a mother. They are rangi and papa, heaven and earth. The earth, out of which all things are produced, is our mother; the protecting and overruling heaven is our father.

It is thus evident that the doctrine of the reciprocal principles of nature, or nature active and passive, male and female, was recognized in nearly all the primitive religious systems of the old as well as of the new world, and in none more clearly than in those of Central America; thus proving, not only the wide extent of the doctrine, but also its separate and independent origin, springing from those innate principles which are common to human nature in all climes and races. Hence the almost universal reverence paid to the images of the sexual parts, as they were regarded as symbols and types of the generative and productive principles in nature, and of those gods and goddesses who were the representatives of the same principles. The Phallus and the Cteis, the Lingam and the Yoni—the special parts contributing to generation and production, becoming thus symbols of those active and passive causes, could not but become objects of reverence and worship. The union of the two symbolized the creative energy of all nature; for almost all primitive religion consisted in the reverence and worship paid to nature and its operations.

Evidence that this worship extensively prevailed will be found in many countries, both in ancient and modern times. It occurs in ancient Egypt, in India, in Syria, in Babylon, among the Assyrians, in Persia, Greece, Italy, Spain, Germany, Scandinavia, and among the Gauls. In Egypt, the phallus is frequently represented as the symbol of generation. According to Ptolemy, the phallus was the object of religious worship among the Assyrians and also among the Persians. In Syria, Baal-Peor was represented with a phallus in his mouth, according to St. Jerome. The Jews did not escape this worship; and we see their women manufacturing phalli of gold and of silver, as we find in Ezekiel xvi. 17.* Among the Hindoos a religious reverence was paid to the Lingam and Yoni,

* "Thou didst take also thy fair jewels of my gold, and didst make to thyself images of men, and didst commit fornication with them."—*Noyes's Translation of Ezekiel.*

and among the Greeks and Romans to the Phallus and Cteis. Among the Teutons and Scandinavians, the god Fricco, corresponding to the Priapus of the Romans, was adored under the form of a phallus; a similar god under a similar symbol was adored in Spain, whose name was Hortanes.

This worship has been found in different parts of America, in Mexico, in Peru, at Hayti; it still prevails at the present day in a great part of India and Thibet. According to Mr. Stephens, the upright pillar in front of the temples of Yucatan is a phallus. We read in an ancient document written by one of the companions of Fernando Cortez: "In certain countries, and particularly at Panuco, they adore the phallus (il membro che portano gli nomini fra le gambe), and it is preserved in the temples." The inhabitants of Tlascala also paid worship to the sexual organs of a man and woman. In Peru, several representations in clay of the phallus are met with. At Hayti, according to Mr. Artaud, phalli have been discovered in different parts of the island, and are believed to be undoubtedly the manufacture of the original inhabitants of the island. In one of the Marianne islands of the Pacific Ocean, on festive occasions, a phallus, highly ornamented, called by the natives Tinas, is carried in procession.

Among the simple and primitive races of men, the act of generation was considered as no more than one of the operations of nature contributing to the reproduction of the species, as in agriculture the sowing of seed for the production of corn, and was consequently looked upon as a solemn duty consecrated to the Deity; as Payne Knight remarks, it was considered as a solemn sacrament in honor of the Creator.

In those early ages, all the operations of nature were consecrated to some divinity, from whom they were supposed to emanate; thus the sowing of seed was presided over by Ceres.

In Egypt, the act of generation was consecrated to Khem; in Assyria, to Vul; in India, to Siva; in Greece, in the primitive pastoral age, to Pan; and in later times, to Priapus; and in Italy, to Mutinus. Among the Mexicans, the god of generation was named Triazoltenti. These gods became the representatives of the generative or fructifying powers in man and nature.

The following curious passage, from Cook's First Voyage, will show that almost similar views were entertained by a primitive race in the islands of the Pacific Ocean, which must have been suggested independently, from their complete disconnection with the ancient world:

"On the 14th I directed that divine service should be performed at the fort: we were desirous that some of the principal Indians should be present, but when the hour came, most of them returned home. Mr. Banks, however, crossed the river, and brought back Tubourai Tamaide and his wife Tomio, hoping that it would give occasion to some inquiries on their part, and some instruction on ours: having seated them, he placed himself between them, and during the whole service, they very attentively observed his behavior, and very exactly imitated it; standing, sitting, or kneeling, as they saw him do; they were conscious that we were employed about somewhat serious and important, as appeared by their calling to the Indians without the fort to be silent; yet when the service was over, neither of them asked any questions, nor would they attend to any attempt that was made to explain what had been done.

"Such were our motives; our Indians thought fit to perform vespers of a different kind. . A young man, near six feet high, performed the rites of Venus with a little girl about eleven or twelve years of age, before several of our people and a great number of the natives, without the least sense of being indecent or improper; but, as appeared, in perfect conformity to the custom of the place. Among the spectators were several women of superior rank, particularly Oberea, who may properly be said to have assisted at the ceremony."*

* Hawkesworth's *Voyages*, vol. i. ch. 12.

The reverence, as well as worship, paid to the phallus in the early ages had nothing in it which partook of indecency: all ideas connected with it were of a reverential and religious kind. When Abraham, as mentioned in Genesis, in asking his servant to take a solemn oath, makes him lay his hand on his parts of generation (in the common version, "under his thigh" *), it was that he required as a token of his sincerity his placing his hand on the most revered part of his body; as, at the present day, a man would place his hand on his heart in order to evince his sincerity. Jacob, when dying, makes his son Joseph perform the same act. A similar custom is still retained among the Arabs at the present day. An Arab, in taking a solemn oath, will place his hand on his membrum virile in attestation of his sincerity.†

The indecent ideas attached to the phallic symbol were, though it seems a paradox to say so, the result of a more advanced civilization verging towards its decline, as we have evidence at Rome and Pompeii. ‡

We may here introduce an extremely just and apposite remark of Constant in his work on Roman polytheism: "Indecent rites may be practised by a religious people with the greatest purity of heart. But when incredulity has gained a footing among these peoples, these rites become then the cause and pretext of the most revolting corruption." A similar remark has been made by Voltaire. Speaking of the worship of Priapus, he says, "Our ideas of propriety lead us to suppose that a ceremony which appears to us so infamous could only be invented by licentiousness; but it is impossible to believe that

---

* The thigh had a peculiar sanctity. It was the part burned of the sacrificial victim as of a sweet savor to the Deity. Bacchus, it will be remembered, was preserved in embryo at the thigh of Jupiter; and Pythagoras, in his initiations, displayed a golden thigh as the last mystery.

† *Mémoires sur l'Egypte*, partie deuxième, p. 196.

‡ *Secret Museum of Naples;* Being an account of the Erotic Paintings, Bronzes, and Statues contained in that famous "Cabinet Secret." By Colonel Fanin. Now first translated from the French. With sixty illustrations. 4to, London, 1871.

Fig. 1.

ROUND TOWER OF IRELAND.

Fig. 2.

OSIRIS SWEARING BY HIS DIVINE POWER.

depravity of manners would ever have led among any people to the establishment of religious ceremonies. It is probable, on the contrary, that this custom was first introduced in times of simplicity, that the first thought was to honor the deity in the symbol of life which it has given us. Such a ceremony may have excited licentiousness among youths, and have appeared ridiculous to men of education in more refined, more corrupt, and more enlightened times."

Three phases in the representation of the phallus should be distinguished; first, when it was the object of reverence and religious worship; secondly, when it was used as a protecting power against evil influences of various kinds, and as a charm or amulet against envy and the evil eye, as at the postern gate at Alatri and at Pompeii, and as frequently occurs in amulets of porcelain found in Egypt, and of bronze in Italy; thirdly, when it was the result of mere licentiousness and dissolute morals. Another cause also contributed to its reverence and frequent representation—the natural desire of women among all races, barbarous as well as civilized, to be the fruitful mother of children—especially as, among some people, women were esteemed according to the number of children they bore, and as, among the Mohammedans of the present day, it is sinful not to contribute to the population; as a symbol, therefore, of prolificacy, and as the bestower of offspring, the phallus became an object of reverence and especial worship among women. At Pompeii was found a gold ring, with the representation of the phallus on its bezel, supposed to have been worn by a barren woman. To propitiate the deity and to obtain offspring, offerings of this symbol were made in Roman temples by women, and this custom has been retained in modern times at Isernia, near Naples. Stone offerings of phalli are also made at the present day in a Buddhist temple in Pekin, and for the same object Mohammedan women kiss with reverence the organ of generation of an idiot or saint. In India this worship has found its most extensive development. There young girls who are anxious for husbands, and married women who are desirous of progeny, are ardent worshippers of Siva; and his symbol, the lingam, is sometimes exhibited in enormous proportions.

In the sixteenth century, St. Foutin in the south of France, St. Ters at Antwerp, and in the last century Saints Cosmo and Damiano at Isernia, near Naples, were worshipped for the same purpose by young girls and barren women.

Sir Gardner Wilkinson records similar superstitious practices at the present day at Ekhmim in Egypt. The superstitions of the natives here ascribed the same properties to a stone in one of the sheikh's tombs, and likewise to that of the temple of Pan, which the statues of the god of generation, the patron deity of Panopolis (Ekhmim), were formerly believed to have possessed; and the modern women of Ekhmim, with similar hopes and equal credulity, offer their vows to these relics for a numerous progeny.

We may conclude with the following passage from Captain Burton, which exhibits similar customs among a rude and barbarous people of the present day: "Among all barbarians whose primal want is progeny, we observe a greater or less development of the phallic worship. In Dahomè it is uncomfortably prominent. Every street from Whydah to the capital is adorned with the symbol, and the old ones are not removed. The Dahoman Priapus is a clay figure, of any size between a giant and the pigmy, crouched upon the ground, as if contemplating its own attributes. The head is sometimes a wooden block rudely carved, more often dried mud, and the eyes and teeth are supplied by cowries. The tree of life is anointed with palm-oil, which drips into a pot or a shard placed below it, and the would-be mother of children prays that the great god Legba will make her fertile."

INFLUENCE OF THE PHALLIC IDEA

IN THE

RELIGIONS OF ANTIQUITY.*

BY C. STANILAND WAKE.

It will not be necessary for me to give details of the rites by which the phallic superstition is distinguished, as they may be found in the works of Dulaure,† Payne Knight,‡ and other writers. I shall refer to them, therefore, only so far as may be required for the due understanding of the subject to be considered—*the influence of the phallic idea in the religions of antiquity.* The first step in the inquiry is to ascertain the origin of the superstition in question. Faber ingeniously referred to a primitive universal belief in a great father, the curious connection seen to exist between nearly all non-Christian mythologies, and he saw in phallic worship a degradation of this belief. Such an explanation as this is, however, not satisfactory; since, not only does it require the assumption of a primitive divine revelation, but proof is still wanting that all peoples have, or ever had, any such notion of a great parent of mankind as that supposed to have been revealed. And yet there is a valuable germ of

---

* A paper read before the Anthropological Society of London, April 5th, 1870.
† *Histoire Abrégé de Différens Cultes*, vol. ii.
‡ *A Discourse on the Worship of Priapus, and its Connection with the Mystic Theology of the Ancients.* By Richard Payne Knight, Esq. New Edition. To which is added An Essay on the Worship of the Generative Powers during the Middle Ages of Western Europe. Illustrated with 138 Engravings. 4to, London, 1869.

truth in this hypothesis. The phallic superstition is founded essentially in the family idea. Captain Richard Burton recognized this truth when he asserted that "amongst all barbarians whose primal want is progeny, we observe a greater or less development of the phallic worship." * This view, however, is imperfect. There must have been something more than a mere desire for progeny to lead primitive man to view the generative process with the peculiar feelings embodied in this superstition. We are, in fact, here taken to the root of all religions—awe at the mysterious and unknown. That which the uncultured mind cannot understand is viewed with dread or veneration, as it may be, and the object presenting the mysterious phenomenon may itself be worshipped as a fetish, or the residence of a presiding spirit. But there is nothing more mysterious than the phenomena of generation, and nothing more important than the final result of the generative act. Reflection on this result would naturally cause that which led to it to be invested with a certain degree of superstitious significance. The feeling generated would have a double object, as it had a double origin—wonder at the phenomenon itself and a perception of the value of its consequences. The former, which is the most simple, would lead to a veneration for the organs whose operation conduced to the phenomena—hence the superstitious practices connected with the phallus and the yoni among primitive peoples. In this, moreover, we have the explanation of numerous curious facts observed among eastern peoples. Such is the respect shown by women for the generative organ of dervishes and fakirs.†

* *Memoirs of the Anthropological Society of London*, vol. 1, p. 320.

† The Vanaprastha were Brahminical anchorites, who inhabited the deserts, lived on vegetables, devoted themselves to contemplation, macerated the body, fought with devils and giants (as a natural consequence), and were insensible to heat and cold. They were called later, by the Greeks, Gymnosophists; and although they went perfectly naked, no throb or involuntary movement was ever seen in any part of their bodies. Women who were barren oftentimes came and touched their shrivelled member, hoping thereby to become fruitful. Not the slightest emotion was noticed at such times.

Such also is the Semitic custom referred to in the Hebrew Scriptures as "the putting of the hand under the thigh," which is explained by the Talmudists to be the touching of that part of the body which is sealed and made holy by circumcision: a custom which was, up to a recent date, still in use among the Arabs as the most solemn guarantee of truthfulness.*

The second phase of the phallic superstition is that which arises from a perception of the value of the consequences of the act of generation. The distinction between this and the preceding phase is that, while the one has relation to the organs engaged, the other refers more particularly to the chief agent. Thus, the father of the family is venerated as the generator; this authority is founded altogether on the act and consequences of generation. We thus see the fundamental importance, as well as the phallic origin, of the family idea. From this has sprung the social organization of all primitive peoples.

An instance in point may be derived from Mr. Hunter's account of the Santals of Bengal. He says that the classification of this interesting people among themselves depends, "not upon social rank or occupation, but upon the family basis." This is shown by the character of the six great ceremonies in a Santal's life, which are: "admission into the family; admission into the tribe; admission into the race; union of his own tribe with another by marriage; formal dismission from the living race by incremation; lastly, a reunion with the departed fathers."†

We may judge from this of the character of certain customs which are widespread among primitive peoples, and the phallic origin of which has long been lost sight of. The value set on the results of the generative act

---

The old ascetics would have regarded with contempt the practices of Christian monks, who were indeed children when compared with their Eastern ancestors.—*The Monks before Christ*, by John Edgar Johnson; and *Description of the Character, Manners and Customs of the People of India*, by Abbé J. A. Dubois.

* See Dulaure, *op. cit.*, vol. ii., p. 219.

† *Rural Bengal*, p. 203.

would naturally make the arrival at the age of puberty an event of peculiar significance. Hence, we find various ceremonies performed among primitive, and even among civilized, peoples at this period of life. Often when the youth arrives at manhood other rites are performed to mark the significance of the event.

Marriage, too, derives an importance from its consequences which otherwise it would not possess. Thus, among many peoples it is attended with certain ceremonies denoting its object, or, at least, marking it as an event of peculiar significance in the life of the individual, or even in the history of the tribe. The marriage ceremonial is especially fitted for the use of phallic rites or symbolism; the former, among semi-civilized peoples, often being simply the act of consummation itself, which appears to be looked on as part of the ceremony. The symbolism we have ourselves retained to the present day in the wedding-ring, which must have had a phallic origin, if, as appears probable, it originated in the Samothracian mysteries.* Nor does the influence of the phallic idea end with life. The veneration entertained for the father of the family as the "generator," led in time to peculiar care being taken of the bodies of the dead; and, finally, to the worship of ancestors, which, under one form or another, distinguished all the civilized nations of antiquity, as it does even now most of the peoples of the heathen world.

CIRCUMCISION.

There is one phallic rite which, from its nature and wide range, is of peculiar importance. I refer to circumcision. The origin of this custom has not yet, so far as I am aware, been satisfactorily explained. The idea that, under certain climatic conditions, circumcision is necessary for cleanliness and comfort, does not appear to be well-founded, as the custom is not universal even within the tropics. Nor is the reason given by Captain Richard

---

* See Ennemoser's *History of Magic* (Bohn). vol. ii, p. 33.

Burton, in his "Notes connected with the Dahoman," for both circumcision and excision, perfectly satisfactory. The real origin of these customs has been forgotten by all peoples practising them ; and, therefore, they have ceased to have their primitive significance. That circumcision, at least, had a superstitious origin may be inferred from the traditional history of the Jews. The old Hebrew writers, persistent in their idea that they were a peculiar people, chosen by God for a special purpose, asserted that this rite was instituted by Jehovah as a sign of the covenant between Him and Abraham. Although we cannot doubt that this rite was practised by the Egyptians and Phœnicians long before the birth of Abraham,* yet two points connected with the Hebrew tradition are noticeable. These are, the religious significance of the act of circumcision—it is the sign of a covenant between God and man—and its performance by the head of the family. These two things are, indeed, intimately connected; since, in the patriarchal age, the father was always the priest of the family and the offerer of the sacrifices. We have it, on the authority of the Veda, that this was the case also among the primitive Aryan people.†
Abraham, therefore, as the father and priest of the family, performed the religious ceremony of circumcision on the males of his household.

Circumcision, in its inception, is a purely phallic rite, having for its aim the marking of that which from its associations is viewed with peculiar veneration, and it connects the two phases of this superstition which have for their object respectively the *instrument* of generation and the *agent*. We are thus brought back to the consideration of the simplest form of phallic worship, that

---

* Herodotus, *Euterpe*, § 104. It was a practice at least 2,400 years before our era, and is even then an ancient custom. Nevertheless it appears to have been found only among nations cognate with the Egyptians and the Phœnicians. The neglect of it by Moses and by the Israelites whom he conducted to the border of the land of Canaan, is a strong presumption against its previous employment by the patriarchs.—*Ed*.

† See Bunsen's *God in History*, vol. 1, p. 299.

which has reference to the generative organs viewed as the mysterious instruments in the realization of that keen desire for children which distinguishes all primitive peoples. This feeling is so nearly universal that it is a matter of surprise to find the act by which it is expressed signalized as sinful. Yet such is the case, although the incidents in which the fact is embodied are so veiled in figure that their true meaning has long been forgotten. Clemens Alexandrinus tells us that " the Bacchanals hold their orgies in honor of the frenzied Bacchus, celebrating their sacred frenzy by the eating of raw flesh, and go through the distribution of the parts of butchered victims, crowned with snakes, shrieking out the name of that Eve, by whom error came into the world." He adds that " the symbol of the Bacchic orgies is a consecrated serpent," and that according to the strict interpretation of the Hebrew term, the name Hevia, aspirated, signifies a *female serpent.** We have here a reference to the supposed fall of man from pristine "innocence," Eve and the serpent being very significantly introduced in close conjunction, and indeed becoming in some sense identified with each other. In fact the Arabic word for serpent, *hayyat,* may be said also to mean "life," and in this sense the legendary first human mother is called Eve or *Chevvah,* in Arabic *Hawwa.* In its relations, as an asserted fact, the question of the fall has an important bearing on the subject before us. Quite irrespective of the impossibility of accepting the Mosaic cosmogony as a divinely inspired account of the origin of the world and man—a cosmogony which, with those of all other Semitic peoples, has a purely "phallic" basis †—the whole transaction said to have taken place in the Garden of Eden is fraught with difficulties on the received interpretation. The very idea on which it is founded—the placing by God, in the way of Eve, of a temptation which He knew she could

---

* *Ante-Nicene Christian Library*, vol. IV. (Clement of Alexandria), p. 27.
† The Hebrew word *bara*, translated "created," has also the sense of "begotten." See Gesenius.

From Kœmpfer.

From Le Bruyn.

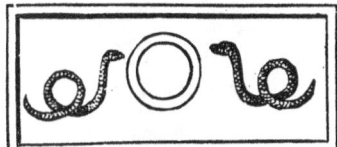
A Chinese Device.
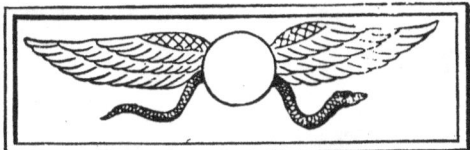
From the Ruins of Naki Rustan.

From the Isiac Table.

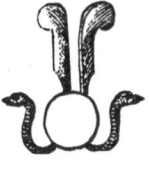

SERPENT-SYMBOLS FOUND IN PERSIA, CHINA, AND EGYPT.

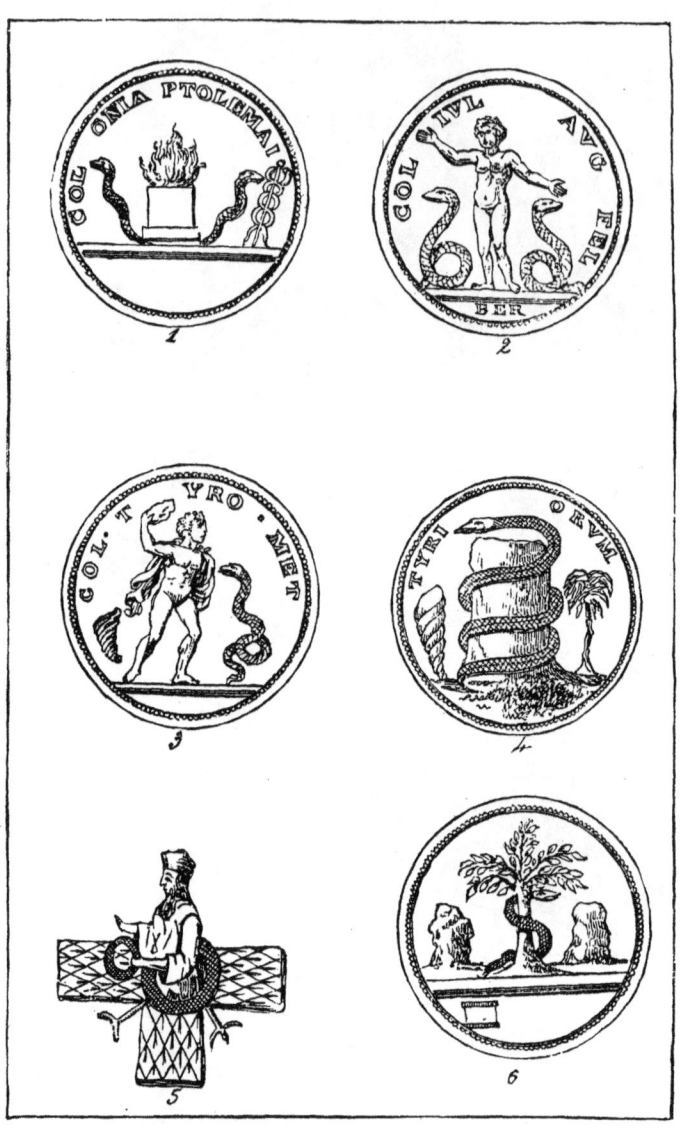

1. FIRE ON THE ALTAR AND SERPENTS REPRESENTING THE TRIAD.
2. THE TRIAD REPRESENTED BY A HUMAN FIGURE AND SERPENTS.
3. THE TRIAD REPRESENTED BY A HUMAN FIGURE, A CONCHA AND SERPENT.
4. THE TRIAD REPRESENTED BY THE SERPENT, THE CONCHA, AND MATERNAL SYMBOL.
5. THE MITHIAIC FIGURE OF AZON, A HUMAN FIGURE ENCIRCLED WITH A ZONE COMPOUND OF A SERPENT.
6. THE TREE OF WISDOM ENCIRCLED BY THE SERPENT, SYMBOLIZING THE MALE AND FEMALE CREATIVE PRINCIPLES.

not resist—is sufficient to throw discredit on the ordinary reading of the narrative. The effect, indeed, that was to follow the eating of the forbidden fruit, appears to an ordinary mind to furnish the most praiseworthy motive for not obeying the command to abstain. That "eating of the forbidden fruit" was simply a figurative mode of expressing the performance of the act necessary to the perpetuation of the human race—an act which in its origin was thought to be the source of all evil—is evident from the consequences which followed, and from the curse it entailed.* As to the curse inflicted on Eve, it has always been a stumbling-block in the way of commentators. For, what connection is there between the eating of a fruit and sorrow in bringing forth children? The meaning is evident, however, when we know that conception and child-bearing were the direct consequences of the act forbidden. How far this meaning was intended by the compiler of the Mosaic books we shall see further on.

SERPENT SYMBOLISM ASSOCIATED WITH PHALLIC WORSHIP.

That we have, in the Mosaic account of the "fall," a phallic legend, is evident from other considerations connected with the narrative. The most important relate to the introduction of the serpent on the scene, and the position it takes as the inciting cause of the sinful act. We are here reminded of the passage already quoted from Clemens Alexandrinus, who tells us that the serpent was the special symbol of the worship of Bacchus. Now, this animal holds a very curious place in the religions of the civilized peoples of antiquity. Although, in consequence of the influence of later thought, it came to be treated as the personification of evil, and as such appears in the Hebrew legend of the fall, yet before this the serpent was the symbol of wisdom and healing. In the latter capacity it appears even in connection with the exodus from Egypt. It is, however, in its character as a symbol of

* See *Jashar*, by Dr. Donaldson, 2d edition (1860), p. 45 et seq.

wisdom that it more especially claims our attention, although these ideas are intimately connected—the power of healing being merely a phase of wisdom. From the earliest times of which we have any historical notice, the serpent has been connected with the gods of wisdom. This animal was the especial symbol of *Thoth* or *Taaut*, a primeval deity of Syro-Egyptian mythology,* and of all those gods, such as *Hermes* and *Seth*, who can be connected with him. This is true also of the third member of the primitive Chaldean triad, *Héa* or *Hoa*. According to Sir Henry Rawlinson, the most important titles of this deity refer " to his functions as the source of all knowledge and science." Not only is he "the intelligent fish," but his name may be read as signifying both "life" and a "serpent," and he may be considered as "figured by the great serpent which occupies so conspicuous a place among the symbols of the gods on the black stones recording Babylonian benefactions." † The serpent was also the symbol of the Egyptian *Kneph*, who resembled the *Sophia* of the Gnostics, the Divine Wisdom. This animal, moreover, was the *Agathodæmon* of the religions of antiquity—the giver of happiness and good fortune.‡ It was in these capacities, rather than as having a phallic significance, that the serpent was associated with the sun-gods, the Chaldean *Bel*, the Grecian *Apollo*, and the Semitic *Seth*.

But whence originated the idea of the wisdom of the serpent which led to its connection with the legend of the "fall"? This may, perhaps, be explained by other facts which show also the nature of the wisdom here intended. Thus, in the annals of the Mexicans, the first woman, whose name was translated by the old Spanish writers

---

* Bunsen's *Egypt*, vol. iv., pp. 225, 255, 288.

† *History of Herodotus*, vol. i., p. 600.

‡ Wilkinson's *Ancient Egyptians*, vol. iv., pp. 412, 413 ; and King's *Gnostics*, p. 31. See also Bryant's *Ancient Mythology*, vol. iv., p. 201. The last named work contains much curious information as to the extension of serpent-worship.

"*the woman of our flesh,*" is always represented as accompanied by a great male serpent. This serpent is the Sun-god *Tonacatl-coatl*, the principal deity of the Mexican pantheon; and the goddess-mother of primitive man is called *Cihua-Cohuatl*, which signifies *woman of the serpent*.* According to this legend, which agrees with that of other American tribes, a serpent must have been the father of the human race. This notion can be explained only on the supposition that the serpent was thought to have had at one time a human form. In the Hebrew legend the tempter speaks; and "the old serpent having two feet," of Persian mythology, is none other than the evil spirit Ahriman himself.† The fact is that the serpent was only a symbol, or at most an embodiment, of the spirit which it represented, as we see from the belief of certain African and American tribes, which probably preserves the primitive form of this supposition. Serpents are looked upon by these peoples as embodiments of their departed ancestors, ‡ and an analogous notion is entertained by various Hindu tribes. No doubt the noiseless movement and the activity of the serpent, combined with its peculiar gaze and marvellous power of fascination, led to its being viewed as a spirit-embodiment, and hence also as the possessor of wisdom.§ In the spirit-character ascribed to the serpent, we have the explanation of the association of its worship with human sacrifice noted by Mr. Fergusson—this sacrifice being really connected with the worship of ancestors.

It is evident, moreover, that we may find here the ori-

---

* See *The Serpent Symbol in America*, by E. G. Squier, M.A. (American Archæological Researches, No. 1, 1851), p. 161 et seq.; *Palenqué*, by M. de Waldeck and M. Brasseur de Bourbourg (1866), p. 48.

† Lajard, *Mémoires de l'Institut Royal de France* (Acad. des Inscriptions et Belles-Lettres), t. xiv., p. 89.

‡ Wood's *Natural History of Man*, vol. i., p. 185; also Squier's *Serpent Symbol*, p. 222 et seq.

§ I have a strong suspicion that, in its primitive shape, the Hebrew legend, as that of the Mexicans, gave the serpent-form to both the father and the mother of the human race.

gin of the idea of evil sometimes associated with the serpent-god. The Kafir and the Hindu, although he treats with respect any serpent which may visit his dwelling, yet entertains a suspicion of his visitant. It may, perhaps, be the embodiment of an *evil* spirit, or for some reason or other it may desire to injure *him*. Mr. Fergusson states that "the chief characteristic of the serpents throughout the east in all ages seems to have been their power over the wind and rain," which they gave or withheld according to their good or ill-will towards man.* This notion is curiously confirmed by the title given by the Egyptians to the Semitic god *Seti* (*Seth*)-*Typhon*, which was the name of the Phœnician evil principle, and also of a destructive wind, thus having a curious analogy with the "typhoon" of the Chinese seas.† When the notion of a duality in nature was developed, there would be no difficulty in applying it to the symbols or embodiments by which the idea of wisdom was represented in the animal world. Thus, there came to be, not only good, but also bad, serpents, both of which are referred to in the narrative of the Hebrew exodus, but still more clearly in the struggle between the good and the bad serpents of Persian mythology, which symbolized Ormuzd, or Mithra, and the evil spirit Ahriman.‡ So far as I can discover, the serpent-symbol has not a *direct* phallic reference,§ nor, after all, is its attribute of wisdom the most essential. The idea most intimately associated with this animal was *life*, not present, but future, and ultimately, no doubt, *eternal.*‖ Thus the snake *Bai* was figured as guardian

* *Tree and Serpent Worship*, p. 46. Rudra, the Vedic form of Siva, the "King of Serpents," is called the father of the maruts (winds). See *infra* as to identification of Siva with Saturn.

† The idea of *circularity* appears to be associated with both these names. See Bryant, *op. cit.*, vol. iii., p. 164, and vol. ii., p. 191, as to derivation of "Typhon."

‡ Lajard, *loc. cit.*, p. 182. See also *Culte de Mithra*, p. 35.

§ In the *Bacchanalia* the serpent's head is seen at the open lid of the box. See Dom. Martin's "*Explication*," etc., pl. II., p. 29.

‖ "Wise φρονιμοι (*phronimoi*) as *serpents*, and harmless (or pure) as *doves*."

of the doorways of those chambers of Egyptian tombs which represented the mansions of heaven.* A sacred serpent appears to have been kept in all the Egyptian temples, and we are told that "many of the subjects, in the tombs of the kings at Thebes in particular, show the importance it was thought to enjoy in a future state." † The use of crowns formed of the asp, or sacred *Thermuthis*, given to sovereigns, and divinities, particularly to Isis,‡ the goddess of life and healing, was, doubtless, intended to symbolize eternal life. This notion is quite consistent with the ideas entertained by the Phœnicians as to the serpent, which they supposed to have the quality "of putting off its old age, and assuming a second youth." §

THE TREE OF KNOWLEDGE OF GOOD AND EVIL.

Another feature of the Mosaic legend of the "fall" which deserves consideration is the reference to the tree of knowledge, or wisdom. It is now generally supposed that the forbidden fruit was a kind of *citrus*, ‖ but certain facts connected with *arborolatry* seem to me to disprove this opinion. Among peoples in the most opposite regions various species of the fig-tree are held sacred. Thus it is, throughout nearly the whole of Africa, with the *banyan* (*Ficus indicus*), the sacred tree of the Hindu Brahmins. Even in several of the Polynesian islands, as in various parts of the Indian Archipelago and in Northern Australia, the fig-tree is highly venerated. In ancient Egypt, the banyan, or the *Ficus sycamorus*, was always considered sacred.¶ So it was in Greece and Italy. Ac-

—Matthew x. 16. By serpents the masculine and by doves the feminine attribute are represented.

* See *Mémoires de l'Institut* (Académie des Inscriptions), tom. xvii., p. 97.
† Wilkinson's *Ancient Egyptians*, vol. v., p. 65.
‡ Do., p. 243.
§ *Sanchoniathon* (translated by Cory), in *The Phœnix*, p. 197.
‖ Smith's *Dictionary of the Bible*. Art., "Apple-Tree."
¶ Wilkinson, *op. cit.*, vol. iv., pp. 260, 313.

cording to Plutarch, a basket of figs formed one of the chief objects carried in the procession in honor of Bacchus; and the sacred phallus itself appears to have been made of the wood of the fig-tree, as was also the statue of the phallic god Priapus.*

Judging from these facts, and considering that the sycamore was sacred among the Hebrews themselves— its fruit having the significance of the virgin womb †— there can be little difficulty in identifying the fig-tree, whether the sycamore or the banyan, with the tree of knowledge planted in the midst of the garden of Eden. The sense intended to be conveyed by this expression would be evident enough without the introduction of the "tree of life." That this is intended to represent the male element is undoubted. The Chaldean god Héa, who was symbolized by the serpent, was also the god of life and knowledge; and Rawlinson states that "there are very strong grounds indeed for connecting him with the serpent of scripture, and with the Paradisiacal traditions of the tree of knowledge and the tree of life."‡ The bo-tree (*Ficus religiosa*) of the Buddhists is said to derive greater sacredness from its encircling the palm— the Palmyra palm being the *kalpa*-tree, or the "tree of life" of the Hindu paradise.§ This connection is termed by the Buddhists "the bo-tree united in marriage with the palm," and we have in it the perfect idea of generative activity, the combination of the male and female elements. Mr. Fergusson, in accordance with his special theory as to the origin of serpent-worship, thinks that this superstition characterized the old Turanian (by which probably he means Hamitic) empire of Chaldea, while

---

* Horace, 8th Satire. See also Ante-Nicene Library, vol. iv., *Clement of Alexandria*, p. 41.

† See Inman's *Ancient Faiths Embodied in Ancient Names*, vol. i., p. 108. This seems to have been the symbolical signification of the fig throughout the East from the earliest historical period; as the *pomegranate* symbolized the full womb.

‡ *History of Herodotus*, Book i., Appendix, Essay 10, § iv.

§ Tennent's *Ceylon*, vol. ii., p. 520.

tree-worship was more characteristic of the later Assyrian empire.* This opinion is, no doubt, correct; and it means really that the older race had that form of faith with which the serpent was always indirectly connected—adoration of the *male* principle of generation, the primitive phase of which was probably ancestor-worship; while the latter race adored the *female* principle, symbolized by the sacred tree, the Assyrian "grove." The "*tree* of life," however, undoubtedly had reference to the male element, and we may well suppose that originally the *fruit* alone was treated as symbolical of the opposite principle.†

There is still an important point connected with the Hebrew legend which requires consideration—the nature of the protecting *kerub*. That this was merely intended as a symbol of the deity himself, there is every reason to believe, and that the symbol was nothing more than the sacred bull of antiquity, is evident from the description of the kerub given by Ezekiel (chaps. i. and x.).‡ But what was the religious significance of the bull, an animal which it would be easy to prove was venerated by nearly all the peoples of antiquity? It is now well known that the bull symbolized the productive force in nature, and hence it was associated with the sun-gods. The symbolic figure carried in procession during the festival of Osiris and Isis was representative, probably, of the phallus of this animal.§ According to the cosmogony of the Zend-Avesta, Ormuzd, after he had created the heavens and the earth, formed the first being, called by Zoroaster "the primeval bull." This bull was poisoned by Ahriman; but its seed was carried, by the soul of the dying animal, represented as an *ized*, to the moon, "where it is continually purified and fecundated by the warmth and light of the sun, to become the germ of all creatures."

---

* *Op. cit.*, p. 12.
† As to the sacred Indian fig-tree, see Ginguiaut's *Religions de l'Antiquité*, vol. i., p. 149, note.
‡ Faber's *Pagan Idolatry*, vol. i., p. 422; vol. iii., p. 606.
§ See Dulaure, *op. cit.*, vol. ii., p. 32.

At the same time, the material prototypes of all living things, including man himself, issued from the body of the bull.* This is but a developed form of the ideas which anciently were almost universally associated with this animal among those peoples who were addicted to sun-worship. There is no doubt, however, that the superstitious veneration for the bull existed, as it still exists, quite independently of the worship of the heavenly bodies.† The bull, like the goat, must have been a sacred animal in Egypt before it was declared to be an embodiment of the sun-god Osiris. In some sense, indeed, the bull and the serpent, although both of them became associated with the solar deities, were antagonistic. The serpent was symbolical of the *personal* male element, or rather had especial reference to the life of *man*, ‡ while the bull had relation to *nature* as a whole, and was symbolical of the *general* idea of fecundity. This antagonism was brought to an issue in the struggle between Osiris and Seti (Seth), which ended in the triumph of the god of nature, although it was renewed even during the exodus, when the golden calf of Osiris, or Horus, was set up in the Hebrew camp.

The references made to the serpent, to the tree of wisdom, and to the bull in the legend of the "fall," sufficiently prove its phallic character; which was, indeed, recognized in the early Christian church.§ This view is confirmed, moreover, by analogous legends in other mythologies. The Hindu legend approaches very nearly to that preserved in the Hebrew scriptures. Thus, it is said that Siva, as the Supreme Being, desired to tempt Brahmá (who had taken human form), and for this object he dropped from heaven a blossom of the sacred fig-tree. Brah-

* Lajard, *Le Culte de Mithra*, p. 50.
† This superstition is found among peoples—the Kafirs, for instance—who do not appear to possess any trace of planetary worship.
‡ This is evident from the facts mentioned above, notwithstanding the use of this animal as a symbol of *wisdom*.
§ In connection with this subject, see St. Jerome, in his letter on Virginity to Eustochia.

má, instigated by his wife, Satarupa, endeavors to obtain this blossom, thinking its possession will render him immortal and divine; but when he has succeeded in doing so, he is cursed by Siva, and doomed to misery and degradation. Mr. Hardwicke, when commenting on this tradition, adds that the sacred Indian fig is endowed by the Brahmans and Buddhists with mysterious significance, as the tree of knowledge or intelligence.* This legend confirms what I have said as to the nature of the Hebrew tree of knowledge, and also the phallic explanation of the "fall" itself, when we consider the attributes of the tempter of the Hindu story. The Persian legend preserved in the *Boun-dehesch* is, however, still more conclusive. According to this legend *Meschia* and *Meschiané*, the first man and woman, were seduced by Ahriman, under the form of a serpent, and they then first committed "in thought, word, and action, the carnal sin, and thus tainted with original sin all their descendants." †

SOURCE OF THE LEGEND OF THE "FALL OF MAN."

Under the circumstances I have detailed, we can hardly doubt that the legend of the "fall" has been derived from a foreign source. That it could not be original to the Hebrews may, I think, be proved by several considerations. The position occupied in the legend by the serpent is quite inconsistent with the use of this animal symbol by Moses.‡ Like Satan himself even, as the Rev. Dunbar Heath has shown,§ the serpent had not, indeed, a wholly evil character among the early Hebrews. In the second place, the condemnation of the act of generation

---

* *Christ and other Masters*, vol. i., p. 305.

† Lajard, *op. cit.*, pp. 52-60. The destruction of purity in the world by the Serpent Dahâka is stated in the 9th Yaçna, v. 27. We have probably here the germ of the fuller legend, which may, however, have been contained in the lost portion of the Zend-Avesta.

‡ The turning of Aaron's rod into a serpent had, no doubt, a reference to the idea of *wisdom* associated with that animal.

§ *The Fallen Angels*, 1857.

was directly contrary to the central idea of patriarchal history. The promise to Abraham was that he should have seed "numerous as the stars of heaven for multitude;" and to support this notion, the descent of Abraham is traced up to the first created man, who is commanded to increase and multiply.

It is very probable, however, that when the legend was appropriated by the compiler of the Hebrew scriptures it had a moral significance as well as a merely figurative sense. The legend is divisible into two parts—the first of which is a mere statement of the imparting of wisdom by the serpent and by the eating of the fruit of a certain tree, these ideas being synonymous, or, at least, consistent, as appears by the attributes of the Chaldean *Héa*.* The nature of this wisdom may be found in the rites of the Hindu *Sacti Puja*.† The second part of the legend, which is probably of much later date, is the condemnation of the act referred to, as being in itself evil, and as leading to misery and even to death itself. The origin of this latter notion must be sought in the esoteric doctrine taught in the mysteries of Mithra, the fundamental ideas of which were the descent of the soul to earth and its re-ascent to the celestial abodes after it had overcome the temptations and debasing influences of the material life. ‡ Lajard shows that these mysteries were really taken from the secret worship of the Chaldean *Mylitta*; but the reference to " the seed of the woman who shall bruise the serpent's head," is too Mithraic for us to seek for an earlier origin for the special form taken by the Hebrew myth. The object of the myth evidently was to explain the origin of *death*, § from which man was to be delivered by a coming Saviour, and the whole idea is strictly Mithraic, the Per-

---

* See *supra*.

† *Memoirs* of the Anthropological Society of London, vol. ii., p. 264, et seq.; and compare with the Gnostic personification of "truth"; for which see King's *Gnostics and their Remains*, p. 39.

‡ Lajard, *op. cit.*, p. 96.

§ Jehovah threatens *death*, but the Serpent impliedly promises *life*, the former having relation to the *individual*, the latter to the *race*.

sian deity himself being a Saviour-God.* The importance attached to *virginity* by the early Christians sprang from the same source. The Avesta is full of references to "purity" of life; and there is reason to believe that, in the secret initiations, the followers of Mithra were taught to regard marriage itself as impure.†

The religious ideas which found expression in the legend of the fall were undoubtedly of late development,‡ although derived from still earlier phases of religious thought. The simple worship in symbol of the organs of generation, and of the ancestral head of the family, prompted by the desire for offspring and the veneration for him who produced it, was extended to the generative force in nature. The bull, which, as we have seen, symbolized this force, was not restricted to earth, but was in course of time transferred to the heavens, and, as one of the zodiacal signs, was thought to have a peculiar relation to certain of the planetary bodies. This astral phase of the phallic superstition was not unknown to the Mosaic religion. A still earlier form of this superstition was, however, known to the Hebrews, probably forming a link between the worship of the symbol of personal generative power and that of the heavenly phallus; as the worship of the bull connected the veneration for the human generator with that for the universal father.

HERMÆ, TERMINI, PILLARS AND "GROVES."

One of the primeval gods of antiquity was *Hermes*, the Syro-Egyptian *Thoth*, and the Roman *Mercury*. Kircher identifies him also with the god *Terminus*. This is doubtless true, as Hermes was a god of boundaries, and appears, as Dulaure has well shown, to have presided over

* Lajard, *op. cit.*, p. 60, note.
† Several of the Essenes, who appear to have had some connection with Mithraism, taught this doctrine.
‡ It is well known to biblical critics that this legend formed no part of the earlier Mosaic narrative.

the national frontiers. The meaning of the word Thoth, *erecting*, associates it with this fact. The peculiar primitive form of Mercury, or Hermes, was " a large stone, frequently square, and without either hands or feet. Sometimes the triangular shape was preferred, sometimes an upright pillar, and sometimes a heap of rude stones." * The pillars were called by the Greeks *Hermæ*, and the heaps were known as *Hermèan heaps*—the latter being accumulated " by the custom of each passenger throwing a stone to the daily increasing mass, in honor of the god." Sometimes the pillar was represented with the attributes of Priapus.†

The identification of Hermes or Mercury with Priapus is confirmed by the offices which the latter deity fulfilled. One of the most important was that of protector of gardens and orchards, and probably this was the original office performed by Hermes in his character of a " god of the country." ‡ Figures set up as charms to protect the produce of the ground would, in course of time, be used not only for this purpose, but also to mark the boundaries of the land protected, and these offices being divided, two deities would finally be formed out of one. The Greek Hermes was connected also with the Egyptian *Khem*, and no less, if we may judge from the symbols used in his worship, with the Hebrew *Eloah*. Thus, in the history of the Hebrew patriarchs, we are told that when Jacob entered into a covenant with his father-in-law Laban, a pillar was set up, and a heap of stones made, § and Laban said to Jacob, " Behold this heap and behold this pillar, which I have cast betwixt me and thee ; this heap be witness, and this pillar be witness, that I will not pass over this heap to thee, and that thou shall not pass over this heap and this pillar unto me for harm."

---

* Faber's *Pagan Idolatry*.
† See Dulaure, *op. cit.*, vol. i., as to the primeval Hermes.
‡ Smith's *Dictionary of Mythology*. Art. " Hermes."
§ Genesis xxxi. 45 to 53. Jacob called the heap or cairn of stones *Galeed*, a circle, and the statue *Mizpeh*, or a pillar.

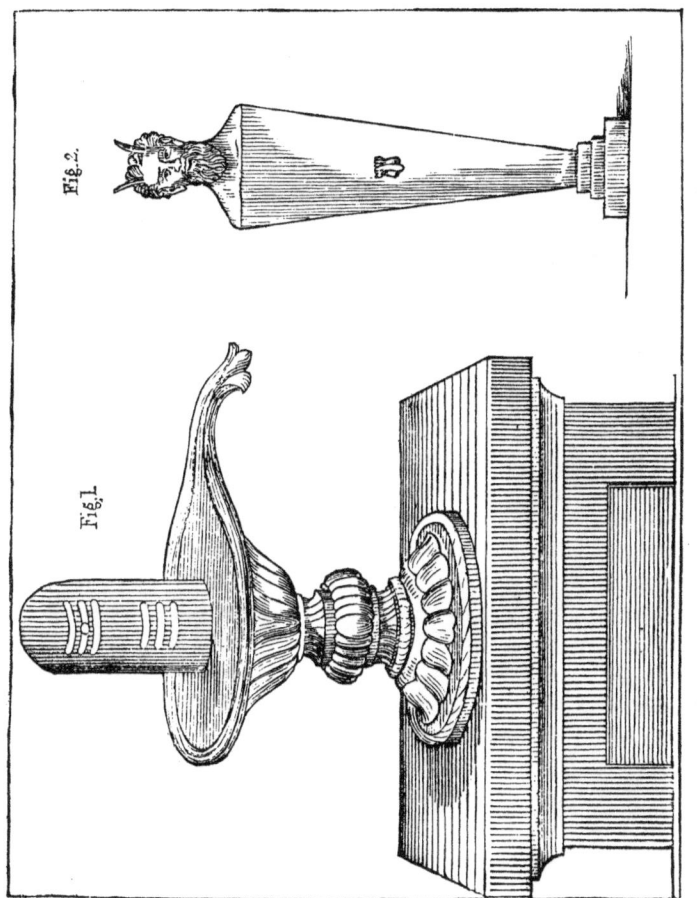

LINGHAM-YONI. PAN'S HEAD.

We have here the *Hermæ* and *Hermean heap*, used by the Greeks as landmarks, and placed by them on the public roads.

In the *linga* of India we have another instance of the use of the pillar-symbol. The form of this symbol is sufficiently expressive of the idea which it embodies—an idea which is more explicitly shown when the Linga and the Yoni are, as is usually the case among the worshippers of the Hindu Siva, combined to form the *Lingam*. The stone figure is not, however, itself a god, but only representative of a spirit * who is thought to be able to satisfy the yearning for children so characteristic of many primitive peoples; this probably having been its original object, and the source of its use as an amulet for the protection of children against the influence of the evil eye. In course of time, however, when other property came to be coveted equally with offspring, the power to give this property would naturally be referred to the primitive phallic spirit, and hence he became, not merely the protector, as we have seen, of the produce of the fields and the guardian of boundaries, but also the god of wealth and traffic, and even the patron of thieves, as was the case with the Mercury of the Romans.

The Hebrew patriarchs desired large flocks as well as numerous descendants, and hence the symbolical pillar was peculiarly fitted for their religious rites. It is related even of Abraham, the traditional founder of the Hebrew people, that he " planted a grove (*eshel*) † in Beersheba, and called there on the name of Jehovah, the everlasting Elohim." ‡ From the phallic character of the "grove" (*ashera*) said to have been in the House of Jehovah, and from the evident connection between the two words, we must suppose that the *eshel* of Abraham also had a phallic

---

* *Linga* means a "sign" or "token." The truth of the statement in the text would seem to follow, moreover, from the fact, that the figure is sacred only after it has undergone certain ceremonies at the hands of a priest.

† Said also to mean a tamarisk tree. It is asserted to have been worshipped in subsequent times.

‡ Genesis xxi. 33.

reference.* Most probably the so-called "grove" of the earlier patriarch, though it may have been of wood, and the stone "bethel" of Jacob, had the same form, and were simply the *betylus*,† the primitive symbol of deity among all Semitic and many Hamitic peoples.

The participation of the Hebrew patriarchs in the rites connected with the "pillar-worship" of the ancient world, renders it extremely probable that they were not strangers to the later planetary worship. Many of the old phallic symbols were associated with the new superstition; and Abraham being a Chaldean, it is natural to suppose that he was one of its adherents. Tradition, indeed, affirms that Abraham was a great astronomer, and, at one time at least, a worshipper of the heavenly bodies; and that he and the other patriarchs continued to be affected by this superstition is shown by various incidents related in the Pentateuch. Thus, in the description given of the sacrificial covenant between Abraham and Jehovah, it is said that, after Abraham had divided the sacrificial animals, a deep sleep fell upon him as the sun was going down, and Jehovah spoke with him. "Then, when the sun went down, and it was dark, behold a smoking furnace and a burning lamp that passed between those pieces." The happening of this event at the moment of the sun's setting reminds us of the Sabæan custom of praying to the setting sun, still practiced, according to Palgrave, among the nomads of Central Arabia.

THE GREAT RELIGIOUS MOVEMENT OF ARCHAIC TIME.

That some great *religious* movement, ascribed by tradition to Abraham, did take place among the Semites at an early date is undoubted. What the object of this

---

* Even if the statement of this event be an interpolation, the argument in the text is not affected. The statement sufficiently shows what was the form of worship traditionally assigned to Abraham.

† "The deity Uranus devised Bætylia, stones having souls" (λιθους εμψυχους —*lithous empsuchous*).

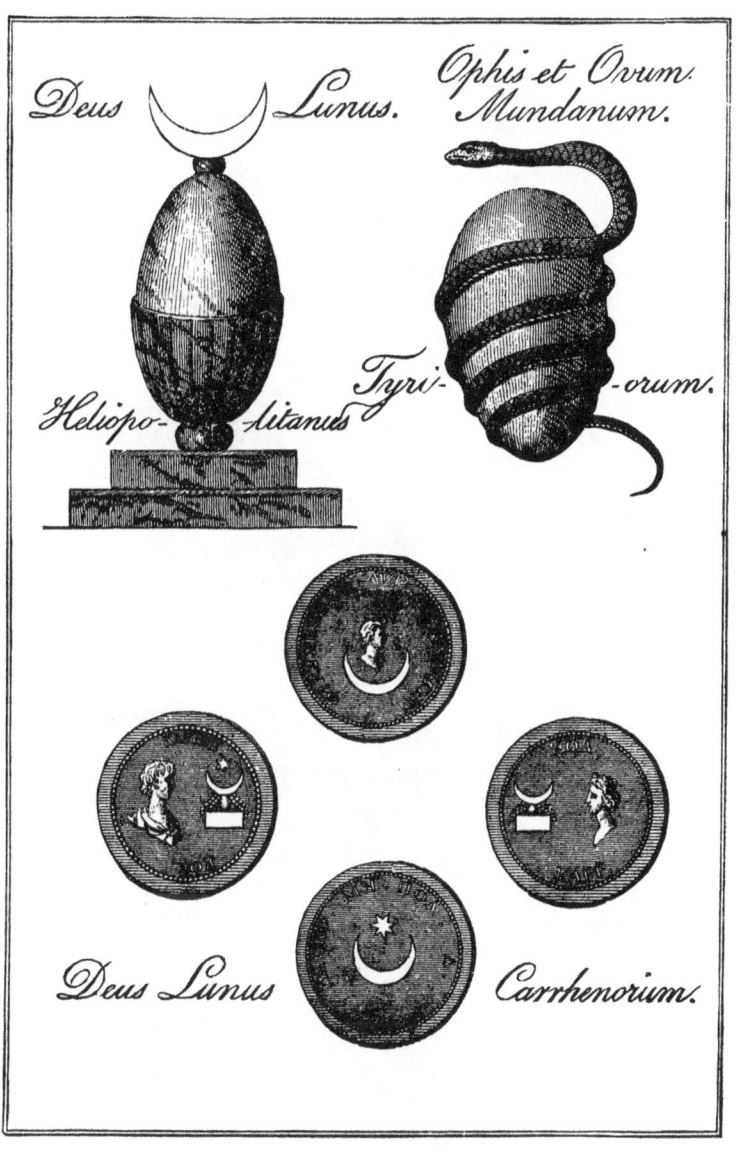

THE MUNDANE EGG OVERSHADOWED BY THE SACRED SERPENT OF ETERNITY.
COINS COMMEMORATIVE OF THE MOON-GOD.

movement was it is difficult to decide.* It should be remembered that the Chaldeans worshipped a plurality of gods, supposed to have been symbolized by the seven planets. Among these deities the sun-god held a comparatively inferior position, the moon-god, *Hurki*, coming before him in the second triad.† It was at Ur, the special seat of the worship of the moon-god,‡ that Abraham is said to have lived before he quitted it for Haran; and this fact, considered in the light of the traditions relating to the great patriarch, may, perhaps, justify us in inferring that the reformation he endeavored to introduce was the substitution of a simple sun-worship for the planetary cult of the Chaldeans, in which the worship of the moon must to him have appeared to occupy a prominent place. The new faith was, indeed, a return to the old phallic idea of a god of personal generation, worshipped through the symbolical *betylus*, but associated also with the adoration of the sun as the especial representative of the deity. That Abraham had higher notions of the relation of man to the divine being than his forerunners is very probable, but his sojourn in Haran proves that there was nothing fundamentally different between his religious faith and that of his Syrian neighbors. I am inclined, indeed, to believe that to the traditional Abraham must be ascribed the establishment of sun-worship throughout Phœnicia and Lower Egypt, in connection with the symbols of an earlier and more simple phallic deity. Tradition, in fact, declares that he taught the Egyptians astronomy; § and we shall see that the religion of the Phœnicians, as, indeed, that of the Hebrews themselves, was the worship of Saturn, the

---

* May it not have been the "Religious War" which is recorded as having taken place in the different countries of the archaic period, from India to the remoter West?—*Ed.*

† Rawlinson's *Five Ancient Monarchies*, vol. i., p. 617; ii., p. 247.

‡ The later Hebrews affected the Persian religion, in which the Sun was the emblem of worship. Abraham evidently had a like preference, being a reputed iconoclast. The lunar religionists employed images in their worship. —*Ed.*

§ Josephus, *Antiquities of the Jews*, Book i., chap. viii., § 2.

erect pillar-god, who, under different names, appears to have been at the head of the pantheons of most of the peoples of antiquity. The reference in Hebrew history to the *teraphim* of Jacob's family recalls the fact that the name assigned to Abraham's father was *Terah*, a " maker of images." The *teraphim* were, doubtless, the same as the *seraphim*, which were serpent-images,* and the household charms, or idols, of the Semitic worshippers of the sun-god, to whom the serpent was sacred.

Little is known of the religious habits of the Hebrews during their abode in Egypt. Probably they scarcely differed from those of the Egyptians themselves; and, even with the religion of Moses, so-called, which we may presume to have been a reformed faith, there are many points of contact with the earlier cult. The use of the ark of Osiris and Isis shows the influence of Egyptian ideas; and the introduction of the new name for God, *Jahvè*, is evidence of contact with late Phœnician thought. † The ark was, doubtless, used to symbolize nature,‡ as distinguished from the serpent- and pillar-symbols which had relation more particularly to man. The latter, however, were by far the most important, as they were most intimately connected with the worship of the national deity, who was the divine father, as Abraham was the human progenitor, of the Hebrew people. That this deity, notwithstanding his change of name, retained his character of a sun-god, is shown by the fact that he is repeatedly said to have appeared to Moses under the figure of a flame. The pillar of fire which guided the Hebrews by night in the wilderness, the appearance of the cloudy pil-

---

* The serpent-symbol of the exodus [Numbers xxi.] is called a "seraph."

† Moses is set forth as the son-in-law of Jethro or Hobab, the Kenite, a priest; and probably became his disciple. At Horeb he learned, by a sacred vision, or initiation, the sacred name. As the Kenites were *scribes* or hierophants (1 Chronicles ii. 55), it is very probable that they had the knowledge of this name, in common with the Phœnicians, Chaldeans, and the sacerdotal orders of other Asiatic nations.—*Ed.*

‡ The ark was the *depositum* of divine or generative power for the preservation of the human race. The dove always accompanies it.

lar at the door of the tabernacle, and probably of a flame over the mercy-seat to betoken the presence of Jehovah, and the perpetual fire on the altar, all point to the same conclusion. The notion entertained by Ewald, that the idea connected with the Hebrew Jahvè was that of a "Deliverer" or "Healer" (Saviour),* is quite consistent with the fact I have stated. Not only was the primeval Phœnician deity, El, or Cronus, the preserver of the world, for the benefit of which he offered a mystical sacrifice,† but "Saviour" was a common title of the sun-gods of antiquity.

THE HEBREW IDENTIFIED WITH ETHNIC RELIGIONS.

There is one remarkable incident which is said to have happened during the wanderings of the Hebrews in the Sinaitic wilderness, which appears to throw much light on the character of the Mosaic cult, and to connect it with other religions. I refer to the use of the brazen serpent as a symbol for the healing of the people.‡ The worship of the golden calf may, perhaps, be described as an idolatrous act, in imitation of the rites of Egyptian Osiris-worship, although probably suggested by the use of the ark. The other case, however, is far different; and it is worth while repeating the exact words in which the use of the serpent-symbol is described. When the people were bitten by the "fiery" serpents,§ Moses prayed for them, and we read that, thereupon, "Jehovah said unto Moses, make thee a fiery serpent [literally, a *seraph*], and set it

* *The History of Israel* (English translation), vol. i., p. 532.
† See *Sanchoniathon* (Cory, *op. cit.*).
‡ "But for the foolish devices of their wickedness, wherewith being deceived, they worshipped serpents void of reason, and vile beasts, thou didst send a multitude of irrational beasts upon them for vengeance, that they might know that wherewithal a man sinneth, by the same also shall he be condemned."—*Wisdom of Solomon*, xi. 16.
§ Much discussion has taken place as to the nature of these animals. For an explanation of the epithet "fiery," see *Sanchoniathon*, "Of the Serpent" (Cory, *op. cit.*).

upon a pole ; and it shall come to pass, that every one that is bitten, when he looketh upon it, shall live. And Moses made a serpent of brass, and put it upon a pole, and it came to pass that, if a serpent had bitten any man, when he beheld the serpent of brass he lived."* It would seem, from this account, that the Hebrew seraph was, as before suggested, in the form of a serpent ; but what was the especial significance of this healing figure ? †

At an earlier stage of our inquiry, I referred to the fact of the serpent being, indirectly, through its attribute of wisdom, a phallic symbol, but also directly an emblem of life, and to the peculiar position it held in nearly all the religions of antiquity. In later Egyptian mythology, the contest between Osiris and the Evil Being, and afterwards that between Horus and Typhon, occupy an important place. Typhon, the adversary of Horus, was figured under the symbol of a serpent, called Aphôphis, or the Giant,‡ and it cannot be doubted that he was only a later form of the god Seth. Professor Reuvens refers to an invocation of Typhon-Seth ; § and Bunsen quotes the statement of Epiphanius that " the Egyptians celebrate the festivals of Typhon under the form of an ass, which they call Seth."‖ Whatever may be the explanation of the fact, it is undoubted that, notwithstanding the hatred with which he was afterwards regarded, this god Seth, or Set, was at one time highly venerated in Egypt. Bunsen says that, up to the thirteenth century before Christ, Set " was a great god universally adored throughout Egypt, who confers on the sovereigns of the eighteenth and nine-

---

* Numbers xxi. 8, 9.

† " Having come to the interior of the desert, the people were exposed to the attacks of *Burning Serpents*, as the original text reads, the bite of which caused great pain ; and not a few of the sufferers died, which again produced an immense excitement in the camp. Moses was ordered to resort to the means of the Phœnician Esculapius, whose symbol, the brass serpent, was erected in the camp, which produced the desired effect."—*History of the Israelitish Nation*, by Isaac M. Wise, p. 102.

‡ Wilkinson's *Ancient Egyptians*, vol. iv., p. 435. § Ditto, p. 434.

‖ *Egypt*, vol. iii., p. 426.

teenth dynasties the symbols of life and power. The most glorious monarch of the latter dynasty, Sethos, derives his name from this deity." He adds: "But subsequently, in the course of the twentieth dynasty, he is suddenly treated as an evil demon, inasmuch that his effigies and name are obliterated on all the monuments and inscriptions that could be reached." Moreover, according to this distinguished writer, Seth "appears gradually among the Semites as the background of their religious consciousness;" and not merely was he "the primitive God of Northern Egypt and Palestine," but his genealogy as "the Seth of Genesis, the father of Enoch (the man), must be considered as originally running parallel with that derived from the Elohim, Adam's father."* That Seth had some special connection with the Hebrews is proved, among other things, by the peculiar position occupied in their religious system by the *ass*—the firstborn of which alone of all animals was allowed to be redeemed†—and the *red heifer*—whose ashes were to be reserved as a "water of separation" for purification from sin.‡ Both of these animals were in Egypt sacred to Seth (Typhon), the ass being his symbol, and red oxen being at one time sacrificed to him, although at a later date objects of a red color were disliked, owing to their association with the dreaded Typhon.§ That we have a reference to this deity in the name of the Hebrew lawgiver is very probable. No satisfactory derivation of this name, Moses, Môsheh (Heb.), has yet been given.‖ Its original form was probably Am-a-ses or Am-ses, which in course of time would become to the Hebrews Om-ses or Mo-ses, meaning only *the* (god) Ses, *i.e.*, Set or Seth.¶ On this

---

* *God in History*, vol. i., pp. 233-4.
† Exodus xxxiv. 20. ‡ Numbers xix. 1-10.
§ As to the God Seth, see Pleyte, *La Religion des Pré-Israélites* (1862).
‖ The Sanscrit, *Maha vusé*, a great sage, seems to be a plausible etymology. *Musa* as it is pronounced, is the Arabic name; and it may have an affinity with the Muses of Thessaly and the ancient sage Musæus.—*Ed.*
¶ According to Pleyte, the Cabalists thought that the soul of Seth had passed into Moses (*op. cit.*, p. 124). It is strange that the name of the

hypothesis, there may have been preserved in the first book of Moses (so-called) some of the traditional wisdom said to have been contained in the sacred books of the Egyptian Thoth, and of the records engraved on the pillars of Seth. It is somewhat remarkable that, according to a statement of Diodorus, when Antiochus Epiphanes entered the temple at Jerusalem, he found in the Holy of Holies a stone figure of Moses, represented as a man with a long beard, mounted on an ass, and having a book in his hand.* The Egyptian mythus of Typhon actually said that Seth fled from Egypt riding on a gray ass.† It is strange, to say the least, that Moses should not have been allowed to enter the promised land, and that he should be so seldom referred to by later writers until long after the reign of David,‡ and above all, that the name given to his successor was Joshua, *i.e.*, *Saviour*. It is worthy of notice that Nun, the name of the father of Joshua, is the Semitic word for *fish*, the phallic character of the fish in Chaldean mythology being undoubted. *Nin*, the planet Saturn, was the fish-god of Berosus, and, as I think can be shown, he is really the same as the Assyrian national deity *Asshur*, whose name and office bear a curious resemblance to those of the Hebrew leader, *Joshua*.

But what was the character of the primitive Semitic deity? Bunsen seems to think that Plutarch, in one passage, alludes to the identity of Typhon (Seth) and Osiris.§ This is a remarkable idea, and yet curiously enough Sir Gardner Wilkinson says that Typhon-Seth may have been

Egyptian princess who is said to have brought up Moses is given by Josephus as *Thermuthis*, this being the name of the sacred asp of Egypt (see *supra*). We appear, also, to have a reference to the serpent in the name Levi, one of the sons of Jacob, from whom the descent of Moses was traced.

* *Fragments*, Book xxxiv. See, also, in connection with this subject, King's *Gnostics*, p. 91.

† Bunsen's *God in History*, vol. i., p. 234.

‡ Ewald notices this fact. See *op. cit.*, p. 454. See, also, Inman's *Ancient Faiths Embodied in Ancient Names*, vol. ii., p. 338.

§ *Egypt*, vol. iii., p. 433.

derived from the pigmy Pthah-Sokari-Osiris,* who was clearly only another form of Osiris himself. However this may be, the phallic origin of Seth can be shown from other data. Thus, it appears that the word *Set* means, in Hebrew, as well as in Egyptian, pillar, and in a general sense, the erect, elevated, high.† Moreover, in a passage of the Egyptian Book of the Dead, Set is called *Tet*, a fact which, according to Bunsen, intimates that Thoth inherited many of the attributes of Set.‡ They were, however, in reality the same deities. Set, by change of the initial letter, becomes *Tet*, one of the names of Thoth, or rather the same name; as Set agrees with Seth.§ We have in this an explanation of the statement that Tet, the Phœnician *Taaut*, was the snake-god Esmun-Esculapius; ‖ the serpent being the symbol of Tet, as we have seen it to have been that of Seth also. In this we have a means of identifying the Semitic deity Seth, with the Saturn and related deities of other peoples. Ewald says that "the common name for God, *Eloah*, among the Hebrews, as among all the Semites, goes back into the earliest times."¶ Bryant goes further, and declares that El was originally the name of the supreme deity among all the nations of the East.** This idea is confirmed, so far as Chaldea is concerned, by later researches, which show that Il or El was at the head of the Babylonian pantheon. With this deity must be identified the Il or Ilus of the Phœnicians, who was the same as Cronus, who again was none other than the primeval Saturn, whose worship appears to have been at one period almost universal among European and Asiatic

---

* *Op. cit.*, vol. iv., p. 434.
† Bunsen's *Egypt*, vol. iv., p. 208.
‡ Ditto, vol. iii., p. 427.
§ As *Tet* becomes *Thoth*, so Mo-*ses* becomes in the Hebrew Mo-*shesh*.
‖ The Brazen Serpent made by Moses, it will be remembered, was the symbol of this divinity; and it was worshipped till the time of King Hezekiah, by whom it was broken in pieces.—*Ed.*
¶ *Op. cit.*, p. 319.
** *Op. cit.*, vol. vi., p. 328.

peoples. Saturn and El were thus the same deity, the latter, like the Semitic Seth, being, as is well known, symbolized by the serpent.* A direct point of contact between Seth and Saturn is found in the Hebrew idol *Kiyun*, mentioned by Amos, the planet Saturn being still called *Kivan* by Eastern peoples. This idol was represented in the form of a pillar, the primeval symbol of deity, which was common undoubtedly to all the gods here mentioned.† These symbolical pillars were called *Betyli*, or *Betulia*. Sometimes also the column was called *Abaddir*, which, strangely enough, Bryant identifies with the serpent-god.‡ There can be no doubt that both the pillar and the serpent were associated with many of the Sun-Gods of antiquity.

Notwithstanding what has been said, it is undoubtedly true that all these deities, including the Semitic Seth, became at an early date recognized as Sun-Gods, although in so doing they lost nothing of their primitive character. What this was is sufficiently shown by the significant names and titles they bore. Thus, as we have seen, *Set* (Seth) itself meant the *erect, elevated, high*, and his name on the Egyptian monuments was nearly always accompanied by the representation of a stone.§ *Kiyun*, or *Kivan*, the name of the deity said by Amos‖ to have been worshipped in the wilderness by the Hebrews, signifies God of the Pillar. The idea embodied in this title is shown by the name *Baal Tamar*, which means " Baal as a Pillar," or " Phallus," consequently " the fructifying God." ¶ The title " erect," when given to a deity, seems always to imply a phallic notion, and hence we have the explanation of the name *S. mou*, used frequently in the

---

* As to the use of this symbol generally, see Pleyte, *op. cit.*, pp. 109, 157.

† On these points, see M. Raoul-Rochette's memoir on the Assyrian and Phœnician Hercules, in the *Mémoires de l'Institut National de France* (*Académie des Inscriptions*), tom. xvii., p. 47 et seq.

‡ *Op. cit.*, vol. i., p. 60; vol. ii., p. 201.

§ Pleyte, *op. cit.*, p. 172.

‖ Chap. v. 26.

¶ Bunsen's *Egypt*, vol. iv., p. 249.

"Book of the Dead," in relation to Thoth, or to Set. There is doubtless a reference of the same kind in the Phœnician myth that "Melekh taught men the special art of erecting solid walls and buildings;" although Bunsen finds in this myth "the symbolical mode of expressing the value of the use of fire in building houses."* That these myths embody a phallic notion may be confirmed by reference to the Phœnician *Kabiri*. According to Bunsen, "the Kabiri and the divinities identified with him are explained by the Greeks and Romans as 'the strong,' 'the great;'" while in the book of Job, *kabbîr*, the strong, is used as an epithet of God. Again, *Sydyk*, the father of the Kabiri, is "the Just, or in a more original sense, the Upright," and this deity, with his sons, correspond to the Phœnician Pataikoi, and to Ptah, their father. Ptah, however, appears to be derived from a root, פתה, which signifies in Hebrew, "to open," and Sydyk himself, therefore, may, says Bunsen, be described as "the opener" of the Cosmic Egg.† The phallic meaning of this title is evident from its application to Esmun-Esculapius (the son of Sydyk) who, as the Snake-God, was identical with Tet, the Egyptian Thoth-Hermes.

The peculiar titles given to these pillar-deities, and their association with the sun, led to their original phallic character being somewhat overlooked, and, instead of being the Father-Gods of human kind, they became *Powerful* Gods, *Lords* of Heaven. This was not the special attribute taken by other sun-gods. I have already stated that Hermes, and his related deities, were "gods of the country," personifying the idea of general natural fecundity. Among the chief gods of this description were the Phœnician *Sabazius*, the Greek *Bacchus-Dionysos*, the Roman *Priapus*, and the Egyptian *Khem*. All these deities agree also in being sun-gods, and as such they were symbolized by animals which were noted either for their fecundity or for their salaciousness. The chief animals thus

* *Egypt*, p. 217.
† See ditto, pp. 226–99.

chosen were the *bull* and the *goat* (with which the ram was afterward confounded *), and this doubtless because they were already sacred. The sun appears to have been preceded by the moon, as an object of worship, but the Moon-God was probably only representative of the primeval Saturn,† who finally became the Sun-God *El* or *Il* of the Syrians and the Semites, and the *Ra* of the Babylonians. The latter was also the title of the Sun-God of Egypt, who was symbolized by the obelisk, and who, although his name was added to that of other Egyptian Gods, appears to have been the tutelary deity of the stranger-kings of the 18th dynasty, whom Pleyte,‡ however, declares to have been Set (Sutech).§ We are reminded here of the opposition of Seth and Osiris, which I have already explained as arising from the fact that these deities originally represented two different ideas--*human fecundity* and the *fruitfulness of nature*. When, however, both of these principles became associated with the solar body, they were expressed by the same symbols, and the distinction between them was in great measure lost sight of. A certain difference was, nevertheless, still observable in the attributes of the deities, depending on the peculiar properties and associations of their solar representatives. Thus the powerful deity of Phœnicia was naturally associated with the strong, scorching summer-sun, whose *heat* was the most prominent attribute. In countries such as Egypt, where the sun, acting on the moist soil left by inundations, caused the earth to spring into renewed life, the mild but energetic early sun was the chief deity.

* It has been suggested that the ram was introduced as an astrological symbol. By the precession of the equinoxes, the sign Aries became the emblem of the Sun, as the genitor of the new year, and so a proper effigy of the Deity. The appearance of the lamb or ram would, of course, create confusion and misapprehension, as well as controversy among those who did not understand astronomy.—*Ed.*

† Rawlinson's *History of Herodotus*, Book i.; appendix, essay x.

‡ Ditto, ii.; appendix, viii. 23.

§ *Op. cit.*, p. 89 et seq.

THE SUN-GODS OF ANTIQUITY.

When considering the sacred bull of antiquity, the symbol of the fecundating force in nature, I referred to Osiris, the national sun-god of the Egyptians, as distinguished from the Semitic Seth (Set), who was identified with the detested Shepherd race. The association of Osiris with Khem shows his phallic character,[*] and, in fact, Plutarch asserts that he was everywhere represented with the phallus exposed.[†] The phallic idea enters, moreover, into the character of all the chief Egyptian deities. Bunsen says: "The mythological system obviously proceeded from 'the concealed god,' Ammon, to the creating god. The latter appears first of all as the generative power of nature in the phallic god Khem, who is afterwards merged in Ammon-ra. Then sprung up the idea of the creative power in Kneph. He forms the divine limbs of Osiris (the primeval Soul) in contradiction to Ptah, who, as the strictly demiurgic principle, forms the visible world. Neith is the creative principle, as nature represented under a feminine form. Finally, her son Ra, Helios, appears as the last of the series, in the character of father and nourisher of terrestrial things. It is he whom an ancient monument represents as the demiurgic principle, creating the mundane egg."[‡] The name of Ammon has led to the notion that he was the embodiment of the idea of wisdom. He certainly was distinguished by having the human form, but his hieroglyphical symbol of the *obelisk*, and his connection with Khem, show his true nature. He undoubtedly represented the primitive idea of a generative god, probably at a time when this notion of fecundity had not yet been extended to nature as distinguished from man, and thus he would form a point of contact between the later Egyptian sun-gods and the pillar-gods of the

---

[*] Wilkinson, *op. cit.*, vol. iv., pp. 342, 260.
[†] Bunsen's *Egypt*, vol. i., p. 423.
[‡] *Op. cit.*, vol. i., p. 388.

Semites and Phœnicians.* To the Egyptians, as to these other peoples, the sun became the great source of deity. His fecundating warmth or his fiery destroying heat were, however, not the only attributes deified. These were the most important, but the Egyptians, especially, made gods out of many of the solar characters;† although the association of the idea of "intellect" with Ammon-ra must have been of late date, if the original nature of Ammon be what I have suggested.

As man, however, began to read nature aright, and as his moral and intellectual faculties were developed, it was necessary that the solar deities themselves should become invested with co-relative attributes, or that other gods should be formed to embody them. The perception of *light*, as distinct from heat, was a fertile source of such attributes. In the Chaldean mythology, *Vul*, the son of *Anu*, was the god of the air; but his power had relation to the purely atmospheric phenomena rather than to light.‡ The only reference to light I find in the titles of the early deities is in the character ascribed to *Va-lua*, the later *Bar* or *Nin-ip*, who is said to " irradiate the nations like the sun, the light of the gods."§ But this deity was apparently the distant planet Saturn, although it may have been originally the moon, and I would refer to the Aryan mind the perception of light as a divine attribute.‖ Thus the Hindu *Dyaus* (the Greek *Zeus*) is the shining deity—the god of the bright sky. As such, the sun-gods now also become the gods of intellectual wisdom, an attribute which likewise appears to have originated with the Aryan peoples, amongst whom the

---

* In the temple of Hercules at Tyre were two symbolical *steles*, one a pillar, and the other an obelisk. See Raoul-Rochette, *op. cit.*, p. 51, where is a reference to a curious tradition preserved by Josephus, connecting Moses with the erection of columns at Heliopolis.

† Wilkinson, *op. cit.*, vol. iv., p. 299.

‡ Rawlinson's *Herodotus*, Book i.; appendix, essay x.

§ Rawlinson, *op. cit.*, Book i.; appendix, essay x.

‖ *Mau*, the name of the Egyptian God of Truth, certainly signifies "light," but probably only in a figurative sense.

DIANA OR ARTEMIS, THE MOTHER-GODDESS OF EPHESUS.

BHAVANI, CONSORT OF MAHA DEVA, THE MOTHER-GODDESS OF PRE-BRAHMAN INDIA.

Brahmans were the possessors of the highest wisdom, as
children of the sun, and whose Apollo and Athênè were
noble embodiments of this attribute. The Chaldean gods
Héa and *Nebo* were undoubtedly symbolized by the
wedge or arrow-head, which had especial reference to
learning. In reality, however, this symbol merely shows
that they were the patrons of letters or writing, and not
of "wisdom," in its purely intellectual aspect. If the
form of the Assyrian alphabetical character was of phallic
origin,* we have here the source of the idea of a connection between physical and mental knowledge embodied in
the legend of the "fall." In the Persian *Ahurô-Mazdâo*
(the Wise Spirit) we have the purest representation of intellectual wisdom. The book of Zoroaster, the Avesta, is
literally the "Word"—the word or wisdom which was revealed in creation, and embodied in the divine Mithra,
who was himself the luminous sun-god.

LESLEY'S "ARKITE SYMBOLISM."

I have already referred to the similarity between the
symbols of the sun-gods of antiquity and the natural objects introduced into the Mosaic myth of the fall; and it
is necessary now to consider shortly what influence the
phallic principle there embodied had over other portions
of Hebraic theology. The inquiries of Dr. Faber have
thrown great light on this question, although the explanation given by him of the myth of Osiris and of the
kindred myths of antiquity is by no means the correct one.
Finding an universal prevalence of phallic ideas and symbolism, Dr. Faber refers it to the degradation of a primitive revelation of the Great Father of the Universe. The
truth thus taught was lost sight of, and was replaced by
the dual notion of a great father and a great mother—
"the transmigrating Noah and the mundane Ark" of

* The importance ascribed to the mechanical arts may, perhaps, lead us to
look for the formal origin of this character in the "wedge," which was the
chief mechanical power the ancients possessed.

the universal deluge. Noah was, however, only a re-appearance of Adam, and the Ark floating on the waters of the deluge was an analogue of the earth swimming in the ocean of space.* There is undoubtedly a parallelism between the Adam and Noah of the Hebrew legends, as there is between the analogous personages of the other phases of these legends; yet it is evident that, if the deluge never happened, a totally different origin from the one supposed by Dr. Faber must be assigned to the great phallic myth of antiquity. It is absolutely necessary, therefore, to any explanation (other than the phallic one) of the origin of this myth, to establish the truth of the Noachic deluge.† Accordingly, a late American writer has formed an elaborate system of "Arkite Symbolism," founded on the supposed influence of the great deluge over the minds of the posterity of those who survived its horrors. Mr. Lesley sees in this catastrophe the explanation of "phallism," which, "converting all the older Arkite symbols into illustrations of its own philosophical conceptions of the mystery of generation, gave to the various parts and members of the human body those names which constitute the special vocabulary of obscenity of the present day."‡

But the priority of these symbols or conceptions is the question at issue. Did the development of "arkism" precede or follow the superstitions referred to by Mr. Lesley as *Ophism*, *Mithraism*, and *Phallism*, all of which I have shown to embody analogous ideas? If the question of priority is to be determined by reference to the written tradition which furnishes the real ground of belief in a great deluge, it must clearly be given to the phallic superstition; for I have shown, conclusively as I think, that almost the first event in the life of man there narrated is

---

* Faber, *op. cit.*, vol. ii., p. 20.

† Bryant, in his *Ancient Mythology*, has brought together a great mass of materials bearing on this question. The facts, however, are capable of quite a different interpretation from that which he has given to them.

‡ *Man's Origin and Destiny*, p. 339.

purely phallic in its symbolism. Nor is the account of the fall the only portion of the Mosaic history of primitive man which belongs to this category. The Garden of Eden, with its tree of life, and the river which divided into four streams, although it may have had a secondary reference to the traditional place of Semitic origin to which the Hebrews looked back with regretful longing, has undoubtedly a recondite phallic meaning. It must be so if the explanation I have given of the myth of the fall be correct, since the two are intimately connected, and the garden* is essential to the succeeding catastrophe.†

The priority of the phallic superstition over "arkism," is proved, moreover, by the undoubted fact that, even in the traditions of the race to whom we are indebted for the precise details of the incidents accompanying the deluge, the phallic deities of the Hamitico-Semites are genealogically placed long before the occurrence of this event. The Semitic deity Seth is, according to one table, the semi-divine first ancestor of the Semites. Bunsen has shown clearly, also, that several of the antediluvian descendants of the Semitic Adam were among the Phœnician deities. Thus, the Carthaginians had a god Yubal, Jubal, who would appear to have been the sun-god Æsculapius, called "the fairest of the gods;" and so also "we read in a Phœnician inscription Ju-Baal, *i.e.*, beauty of Baal, which Movers ingeniously interprets Æsculapius-Asmun-Jubal." Here, then, adds Bunsen, "is another old Semitic name attached to a descendant of Lamekh, together with Adah, Zillah, and Naamah."‡ Hadah, the wife of Lamekh as well as of Esau, the Phœnician Usov, is identified with the goddess worshipped at Baby-

* Compare this with the figurative description of the garden of delights of "The Song of Songs."

† The Hebrew term גן GN, or garden, appears to be closely related to the Greek word γυνη, *gune*, or woman. Indeed, in the ancient languages the former is used as a metaphor for the latter. See Inman's *Ancient Faiths Embodied in Ancient Names*, vol. i., p. 52; vol. ii., p. 553.

‡ *Egypt*, vol. iv., p. 257.

lon as Hera (Juno), and, notwithstanding Sir Gardner Wilkinson's dictum to the contrary, her names, Hera, Hadah, point to the connection with the Egyptian *Her Her*, or *Hathor*, who was the daughter of Seb and Netpe, as Hera was the daughter of Cronus and Rhea. The name of the god *Kiyun*, or *Kivan*, who was worshipped by the Hebrews, and who in Syria was said to devour children, is connected with the root *kun*, to erect, and therefore doubtless with the antediluvian *Kain* or Kevan. *Kon*, derived from the same root, was, according to Bunsen, a Phœnician designation of Saturn.* Even the great Carthaginian god *Melekh*, who was also held in universal honor throughout all Phœnicia, appears, although Bunsen does not thus identify him, to be no other than Lamekh, the father of Noah.† Ewald, indeed, says that both Lamekh and Enoch were gods or demi-gods, and that Methuselah was a sort of Mars, while Mahahal-el was a god of light, and Jareda a god of the lowland or of the water.‡

The priority of the phallic superstition over Arkism, or rather the existence of that superstition before the formation of the deluge-legend, is proved, moreover, by the agreement of this legend with the myth of Osiris and Isis in its primitive form, while Typhon (Seth) was honored by the Egyptians as a great god.§ Bunsen fixes the origin of this myth in its amended form so late as the thirteenth or fourteenth century B.C.‖ In the face of this agreement we can only suppose the myth and the deluge-legend to have had the same basis—a basis which, from the very circumstances of the case, must be purely "phallic." This explanation is the only one which is

* *Egypt*, p. 209.
† This notion furnishes an easy explanation, founded on the human sacrifices to the Phœnician deity, of the curious verse in Genesis as to the avenging of Lamekh. [The Lamekh here referred to was not father of Noah. Compare Genesis iv. 18-24, with v. 25-29.]
‡ *Op. cit.*, vol. i., pp. 266-7.
§ For explanation of this myth, see Bunsen's *Egypt*, vol. iii., p. 437.
‖ Ditto, p. 413.

consistent with a peculiarity in the Hebrew legend, which is an insurmountable objection to its reception as the expression of a literal fact. We are told by the Mosaic narrative that Jehovah directed Noah to take with him into the Ark "of fowls after their kind, and of cattle after their kind, of every creeping thing of the earth after his kind, two of every sort." Now, according to the ordinary acceptation of the legend, this passage expresses a simple absurdity, even on the hypothesis of a partial deluge. If, however, we read the narrative in a phallic sense, and by the Ark understand the sacred *argha* of Hindu mythology, the Yoni of Parvati, which, like the moon in Zoroastrian teaching, carries in itself the germs of all things, we see the full propriety of what otherwise is incomprehensible. As εν αρχη, [*en arché*] the Elohim created the heavens and the earth, so in the Ark were the seeds of all things preserved that they might again cover the earth. Taken in this sense, we see the reason of the curious analogy which exists in various points between the Hebrew legends of the creation and of the deluge; this analogy being one of the grounds on which the hypothesis of the Great Father as the central idea of all mythologies has been based. Thus, the primeval ship, the navigation of which is ascribed to the mythological being, is not the ark of Noah or Osiris, or the vessel of the Phœnician Kabiri. It was the moon, the ship of the sun, in which his seed is supposed to be hidden until it bursts forth in new life and power. The fact that the moon was in early mythologies a male deity almost necessitates, however, that there should have been another origin for the sacred vessel of Osiris. This we have in the Hastoreth-*karnaim*, the cow-goddess, whose horns represent the lunar ark, and who, without doubt, was a more primitive deity than the moon-goddess herself.*
The most primitive type of all, however, is that of the

---

* Want of space prevents me from tracing the developments which the primeval goddess of fecundity underwent; but to the idea embodied in her may be traced nearly all the female deities of antiquity.

argha or *yoni* of the Indian Iswara, which, from its name, was supposed to have been turned into a dove.* Thus, in Noah and the Ark, as in Osiris and the Moon, we see simply the combination of the male and female elements, as they are still represented in the Hindu lingam. The introduction of the dove into the myth is a curious confirmation of this view. For, this bird, which, as "the emblem of love and fruitfulness," was "consecrated to Venus under all her different names at Babylon, in Syria, Palestine, and Greece† which was the national banner-sign of the Assyrians, as of the earlier Scythic empire, whose founders, according to Hindu tradition, took the name of *Ionim* or *Yoniyas*, and which attended on Janus, a diluvian "God of opening and shutting," was simply a type of "the Yoni or Jonah,‡ or navicular feminine principle," which was said to have assumed the form of a ship and a dove.§

PHALLISM IN THE MODERN RELIGIONS.

In bringing this paper to a close, I would refer shortly to what may be called the modern religions—Brahminism, Buddhism, and Christianity—seeing that these still exist as the faiths of great peoples. As to the first of these, it may be thought that its real character cannot be ascertained from the present condition of Hindu belief. It is said that the religion of the Vedas is very different from that of the Puranas, which have taken their place. It should be remembered, however, that these books profess to reproduce old doctrine, the word "Purana" itself meaning *old*, and that Puranas are referred to in one of

---

* Faber, *op cit.*, vol. ii., p. 246.
† Kenrick's *Phœnicia*, p. 307.
‡ The story of Jonah, the יונה, dove or symbol of femininity, going to Joppa, a seaport where Dag-on the fish-god was worshipped, and having entered a ship is swallowed by a *Ceto* or great fish, betrays a suspicious relationship to the same cultus. The fish was revered at Joppa as the dove was at Nineveh. Was there an esoteric meaning?—*Ed.*
§ Faber's *op. cit.*, and Bryant's *Ancient Mythology*, ii., pp. 317 et seq.

the Upanishads, while the *Tantras*, which contain the principles of the *Sacti Puja*, and which are, as yet, almost unknown to Europeans, are considered by the Brahmans to be more ancient than the Puranas themselves.* The origin of the ideas contained in these books is a difficult question. The germs of both Vishnu-worship and Siva-worship appear to be found in the Vedas,† and are undoubtedly referred to by the Mahabharata.‡ I am inclined to think with Mr. Fergusson and other late writers that they are only indirectly sprung from the primitive Hinduism. The similarity between Sivaism and the Santal worship of the Great Mountain, pointed out by Mr. Hunter, is very remarkable, and this analogy is strengthened by intermixture in both cases with river-worship.§ There is no doubt that the Great Mountain is simply a name for the phallic emblem, which is the chief form under which Siva is represented in the numerous temples at Benares dedicated to his honor.

SERPENT-WORSHIP A VISHNAVIC CUSTOM.

Considering the position occupied by the serpent as a symbol of life, and, indirectly, of the male power, we should expect to find its worship connected to some extent with that of Siva. Mr. Fergusson, however, declares that it is not so; and, although this statement requires some qualification,‖ yet it is certain that the serpent is

* On this question, see the *Memoirs* of the Anthropological Society of London, vol. ii., p. 265; also "Sketch of the Religious Sects of the Hindus," in the *Asiatic Researches*, vol. xvii. (1832), 216 et seq.

† This question is fully considered by Dr. Muir, in his *Sanskrit Texts*, part iv., p. 54 et seq.

‡ Ditto, pp. 161, 343.

§ *Rural Bengal*, pp. 152, 187 et seq. This association of the mountain and the river is found also in the Persian Khordah-Avesta. See (5) Abun-Yasht, v. 1-3.

‖ See *Tree and Serpent Worship*, p. 70; also Sherring's *Benares*, pp. 75, 89. Here the serpent is evidently symbolical of *life*. In the Mahabharata, Mahadeva is described as having "a girdle of serpents, ear-rings of serpents, a sacrificial cord of serpents, and an outer garment of serpent's skin." (Dr. Muir, *op. cit.*, part iv., p. 160.)

also intimately associated with Vishnu. In explanation of this fact, Mr. Fergusson remarks : " The Vaishnava religion is derived from a group of faiths in which the serpent always played an important part. The eldest branch of the family was the Naga worship, pure and simple ; out of that arose Buddhism, . . . and on its decline two faiths—at first very similar to one another—rose from its ashes, the Jaina and the Vaishnava." The serpent is almost always found in Jaina temples as an object of worship, while it appears everywhere in Vaishnava tradition.* But elsewhere Mr. Fergusson tells us that, although Buddhism owed its establishment to Naga tribes, yet its supporters repressed the worship of the serpent, elevating tree-worship in its place. †

It is difficult to understand how the Vaishnavas, who are worshippers of the *female* power,‡ and who hate the *lingam*, can yet so highly esteem the serpent, which has, indirectly at least, reference to the male principle. Perhaps, however, we may find an explanation in Mr. Fergusson's own remarks as to the character and development of Buddhism. According to him, Buddhism was chiefly influential among Naga tribes, and " was little more than a revival of the coarser superstitions of the aboriginal races,§ purified and refined by the application of Aryan morality, and elevated by doctrines borrowed from the intellectual superiority of the Aryan races." ‖ As to its de-

* *Op. cit.*, p. 70.
† Ditto, p. 62.
‡ Mr. Sellon, in the *Memoirs* of the Anthropological Society of London, vol. ii., p. 273.
§ It should not be forgotten that the Vedic religion was not that of all the Aryan tribes of India. (See Muir, *op. cit.*, part ii., p. 377, 368–383) ; and it is by no means improbable that some of them retained a more primitive faith, Buddhism or Rudraism ; *i.e.*, Sivaism. See also Baldwin's *Prehistoric Nations*.

‖ *Op. cit.*, p. 62. To come to a proper conclusion on this important point, it is necessary to consider the real position occupied by Gautama in relation to Brahminism. Burnouf says that he differed from his adversaries only in the definition he gives of Salvation (*du salut*). (*Introduction à l'Histoire du Buddhisme Indien*, p. 155.)

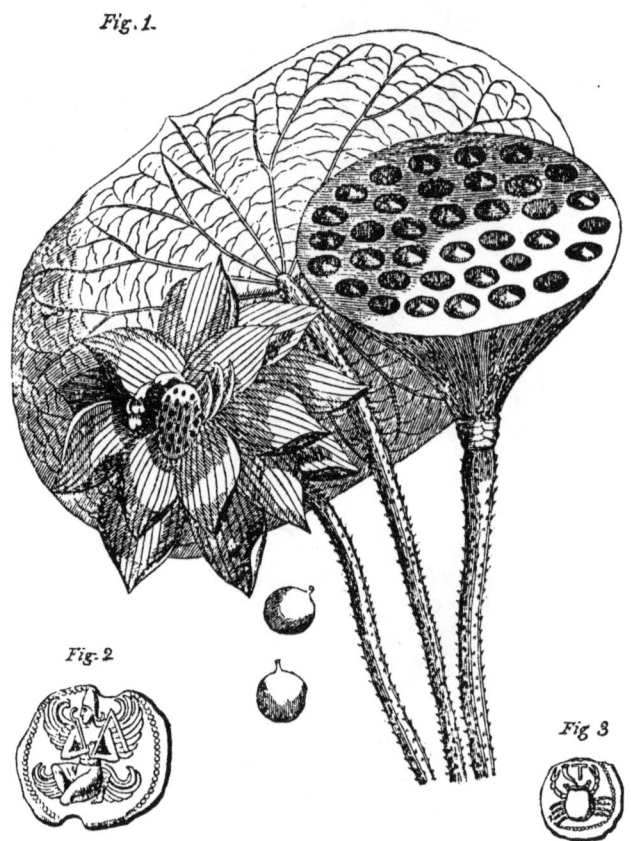

THE SACRED LOTUS-FLOWER.
NYMPHÁEA NELUMBO.
THE FEMALE SYMBOL IN EGYPT, INDIA, AND EASTERN ASIA.

velopment, the sculptures on the Sanchi Topes show that at about the beginning of the Christian era, although the *dagoba*, the *chakra*, or wheel, the *tree*, and other emblems, were worshipped, the serpent hardly appears; while, at Amravati, three centuries later, this animal had become equal in importance to Buddha himself.* Moreover, there can be no doubt that the *lingam* was an emblem of Buddha, as was also the *lotus*, which represents the same idea—the conjunction of the male and female elements, although in a higher sense perfect wisdom.† The association of the same ideas is seen in the noted prayer, *Om mani padmi hum* ("Om, the Jewel in the Lotus"), which refers to the birth of Padmipani from the sacred lotus-flower,‡ but also, there can be little doubt, to the phallus and the yoni. We may suppose, therefore, that, whatever the moral doctrine taught by Gautama, he used the old phallic symbols,§ although, it may be, with a peculiar application. If the opinion expressed by Mr. Fergusson, as to the introduction into India of the Vaishnava faith by an early immigrant race, be correct, it must have existed in the time of Gautama; and, indeed, the Ionism of Western Asia is traditionally connected with India itself at a very early date,‖ although probably the early centre of Ion-ism, the worship of the Dove, or Yoni, was, as Bryant supposes, in Chaldea.¶ We see no trace, however, in Buddhism proper of *Sacti Puja*, and I would suggest that, instead of abolishing either, Gautama substituted for the separate symbols of the linga and the yoni, the association of the two in the *lingam*. If this were so, we can well understand how, on the fall of Buddhism, Siva-worship** may have retained this compound symbol, with

* Fergusson, *op. cit.*, pp. 67, 222, 223.
† See Guigniaut, *op. cit.*, vol. i., pp. 293, 160 *note*.
‡ Schlagenweit, *Buddhism in Thibet*, p. 120.
§ These are figured in the *Journal* of the Royal Asiatic Society, vol. xviii.
‖ Higgins's *Anacalypsis*, vol. i., p. 332 et seq. See also p. 342 et seq.
¶ *Op. cit.*, vol. iii., p. 1 et seq., 25.
** Mr. Hunter points out a connection between Sivaism and Buddhism. *Op. cit.*, p. 194.

many of the old Naga ideas, although with little actual reference to the serpent itself other than as a symbol of life and power ; while, on the other hand, the Vaishnavas may have reverted to the primitive worship of the female principle, retaining a remembrance of the early serpent associations in the use of the *sesha*, the heavenly Naga with seven heads,* figured on the Amravati sculptures. It is possible, however, that there may be another ground of opposition between the followers of Vishnu and Siva. Mr. Fergusson points out that, notwithstanding the peculiarly phallic symbolism of the latter deity, " the worship of Siva is too severe, too stern, for the softer emotions of love, and all his temples are quite free from any allusion to it." It is far different with the Vaishnavas, whose temples " are full of sexual feelings, generally expressed in the grossest terms." †

Siva, in fact, is especially a god of intellect, typified by his being three-eyed, and, although terrible as the resistless destroyer, yet the re-creator of all things in perfect wisdom ; ‡ while Vishnu has relation rather to the lower type of wisdom which was distinctive of the Assyrians among ancient peoples, and which has so curious a connection with the female principle. Hence the *shell*, or *conch*, is peculiar to Vishnu, while the *linga* belongs to Siva.§ Gautama combined the simpler feminine phase of religion with the more masculine intellectual type, symbolizing this union by the lingam and other analogous emblems. The followers of Siva have, however, adopted the combined symbol in the place of the linga alone, thus ap-

* See Mr. Fergusson, *op. cit.*, p. 70. The serpent is connected with Vishnuism as a symbol of *wisdom* rather than of life.

† *Op. cit.*, p. 71.

‡ Hence Siva, as *Sambhu*, is the patron deity of the Brahmanic order ; and the most intellectual Hindus of the present day are to be found among his followers. (See Wilson, *op. cit.*, p. 171. Sherring's *Sacred City of the Hindus*, p. 146 et seq.)

§ The *bull* of Siva has reference to strength and speed rather than to fecundity ; while the Rig-Veda refers to Vishnu as the framer of the womb, although elsewhere he is described as the *fecundator*. (See Muir, *op. cit.*, part iv., pp. 244, 292, also pp. 64, 83.)

proaching more nearly than the Vaishnavas to the idea of the founder of modern Buddhism. Gautama himself, nevertheless, was most probably only the restorer of an older faith, according to which perfect wisdom was to be found only in the typical combination of the male and female principles in nature. The real explanation of the connection between Buddhism and Sivaism has perhaps, however, yet to be given.* The worship of the serpent-god is not unknown, even at the present day, in the very stronghold of Sivaism,† reminding us of the early spread of Buddhism among Naga tribes. In the "crescent surmounted by a pinnacle, similar to the pointed end of a spear," which decorates the roofs of the Tibetan monasteries,‡ we, undoubtedly, have a reproduction of the so-called trident of Siva. This instrument is given also to *Sani*, the Hindu Saturn, who is represented as encompassed by two serpents,§ and hence we may well suppose the pillar-symbol of this primeval deity to be reproduced in the linga of the Indian phallic god.‖

But the pillar-symbol is not wanting to Buddhism itself. The columns said to have been raised by Asoka have a reference to the inscribed pillars of Seth. The remains of an ancient pillar, supposed to be a Buddhist *Lat*, is still to be seen at Benares;¶ the word *Lat* being merely another form of the name *Tet*, *Set*, or *Sat*, given to the Phœnician or Semitic deity. In the central pillar of the so-called Druidical circles, we have, doubtless, a reference to the same primitive superstition, the idea intended to be represented being the combination of the male and female principles.**

* This question has been considered by Burnouf, *op. cit.*, p. 547 et seq. But see also Hodgson's *Buddhism in Nepaul*, and Paper in the *Journal* of the Royal Asiatic Society, vol. 18 (1860), p. 395 et seq.

† See Sherring, *op. cit.*, p. 89.

‡ Schlagenweit, *op. cit.*, p. 181.

§ Maurice's *Indian Antiquities*, vol. vii., p. 566.

‖ As to the identity of Siva and Saturn, see Guigniaut, *op. cit.*, vol. i., p. 167 *note*. *Kivan*, a name of Saturn, is really the same word as *Siva*.

¶ Sherring, *op. cit.*, p. 305 et seq.

** It should be noted that many of the so-called "circles" are in reality *elliptical*.

PHALLISM IN THE CHRISTIAN SYMBOLS.

In conclusion, it must be said that Christianity itself is certainly not without the phallic element. Reference may be made to the important place taken in Christian dogma by the " fall "—which I have shown to have had a purely " phallic" foundation—and to the peculiar position assigned to Mary, as the Virgin Mother of God.* It must not be forgotten, however, that, whatever may have been the primitive idea on which these dogmas are based, it had received a totally fresh aspect, at the hands of those from whom the founders of Christianity received it.† As to symbols, too, these were employed by the Christians in the later signification given to them by the followers of the ancient faiths. Thus, the fish- and the cross-symbols originally embodied the idea of generation, but afterwards that of life, and it was in this sense that they were applied to Christ.‡ The most evidently phallic representation used by the Christian iconographers is undoubtedly the *aureole* or *vessica*. This was generally elliptical in form, and contained the figure of Christ; Mary herself, however, being sometimes represented in the aureole, glorified as Jesus Christ.§ Probably the *nimbus*, also, is of phallic significance; for, although generally circular, it was sometimes triangular, square, etc.‖ The name of Jehovah is inscribed within a radiating triangle.¶ Didron gives a representation of St. John the Evangelist with a circular nimbus, surmounted by two sunflowers, emblems of the sun, an idea which, says Didron, "reminds us of the Egyptian figures, from the heads of which two lotus-

---

* On this subject, see Higgins's *Anacalypsis*, vol. i., p. 315 et seq.

† We must look to the esoteric teaching of Mithraism for the origin and explanation of much of primitive Christian dogma.

‡ The serpent elevated in the Wilderness is said to be typical of Christ. (John iii. 14, 15). A Gnostic sect taught that Christ was Seth.

§ Didron's *Christian Iconography* (Bohn), pp. 272, 286.

‖ It is a curious fact that Buddhist deities are often represented in the *Vessica* and with the nimbus. (See Hodgson's figures, plates v. and vi. in the *Journal* of the Royal Asiatic Society, vol. 18.)

¶ Didron, pp. 27, 231.

flowers rise in a similar manner."* There is also a curious representation, in this work, of the *divine hand*, with the thumb and two forefingers outstretched, resting on a cruciform nimbus (p. 215). In Egypt, the hand having the fingers thus placed was a symbol of Isis, and from its accompaniments, there can be little doubt, notwithstanding the mesmeric character ascribed to it by Ennemoser,† that it had an essentially phallic origin, although it may ultimately have been used to signify life.

There can be no question, however, that, whatever may be thought of its symbols,‡ the fundamental basis of Chris-

---

* Didron, p. 29.
† *History of Magic* (Bohn), vol. i., p. 253 et seq.
‡ The "Black Virgins" of the French cathedrals prove, when examined critically, to be basalt figures of the goddess Isis. The Virgin Mary succeeded to her form, titles, symbols, rites, and ceremonies. Thus the devotees of Isis carried into the new priesthood the former badges of their profession, the obligation to celibacy, the tonsure, and the surplice. The sacred image still moves in procession as when Juvenal laughed at it—vi. 530—"*grege linigero circumdatus et grege calvo*"—escorted by the tonsured, surpliced train. Her proper title, Domina, the exact translation of the Sanscrit *Isi*, survives, with a slight change in the modern Madonna. By a singular permutation, the flower borne by each, the lotus, ancient emblem of fecundity, now renamed the lily, is interpreted as significant of the opposite quality. The tinkling sistrum, a sound so well pleasing to the Egyptian goddess, is replaced by that most hideous of noises, the clattering bell. The latter instrument, however, came directly from the Buddhist religious usages, where it forms as essential an element as of yore in early Celtic Christianity, when the holy bell was the actual type of the Godhead to the new converts. The bell in its present form was unknown to the ancients; its normal shape is Indian, and the first real bell-founders were the Buddhist Chinese. Again, relic-worship seems from the third century to have been virtually the present form of Christianity in the East. A fragment of the bone of a Buddha is indispensable in the founding of a temple of that faith.

It is astonishing how much of the Egyptian and the second-hand Indian symbolism passed over into the usages of the following times. The high cap and hooked staff of the god became the bishop's mitre and crosier; the term *nun* is purely Egyptian, and bore its present meaning; the erect oval, symbol of the Female Principle of Nature, became the Vesica Piscis, and a frame for divine things; the Crux Ansata, testifying the union of the Male and Female Principle in the most obvious manner, and denoting fecundity and abundance, is transformed, by a simple inversion, into the Orb surmounted by the Cross, and the ensign of royalty. (*Gnostics and their Remains*, by C. W. King, pp. 71, 72.)

tianity is more purely "phallic" than that of any other religion now existing. I have referred to the presence in Hebraic theology of an idea of God—that of a Father—antagonistic to the Phœnician notion of the "Lord of Heaven." We have the same idea repeated in Christ's teaching, its distinctive characteristic being the recognition of God as the Universal Father, the Great Parent of Mankind, who had sent His son into the world that he might reconcile it unto Himself. It is in the character of a forgiving parent that Christians are taught to view God, when He is not lost sight of in the presence of Christ. The emotional nature of Christian faith, indeed, shows how intimately it was related to the older faiths which had a phallic basis. In Christianity, we see the final expression of the primitive worship of the father as the head of the family, the generator, as the result of an instinctive reasoning process leading up from the particular to the universal, with which, however, the dogma of the "fall" and its consequences—deduced so strangely from a phallic legend—have been incorporated. The "phallic" is, indeed, the only foundation on which an emotional religion can be based. As a religion of the emotions, therefore, the position of Christianity is perfectly unassailable. As a system of rational faith, however, it is far different; and the tendency of the present age is just the reverse of that which took place among the Hebrews—the substitution of a Heavenly King for a Divine Father. In fact, modern science is doing its best to effect for primitive fetishism, or demon-worship, what Christianity has done for phallic worship—generalize the powers of nature and make of God a Great Unknowable Being, who, like the Elohim of the Mosaic cosmogony, in some mysterious manner, causes all things to appear at a word. This cannot be, however, the real religion of the future. If God is to be worshipped at all, the Heavenly King and Divine Father must be combined in a single term; and he must be viewed, not as the unknowable cause of being, but as the Great Source of all being, who may be known in nature—the expression of his life and energy.

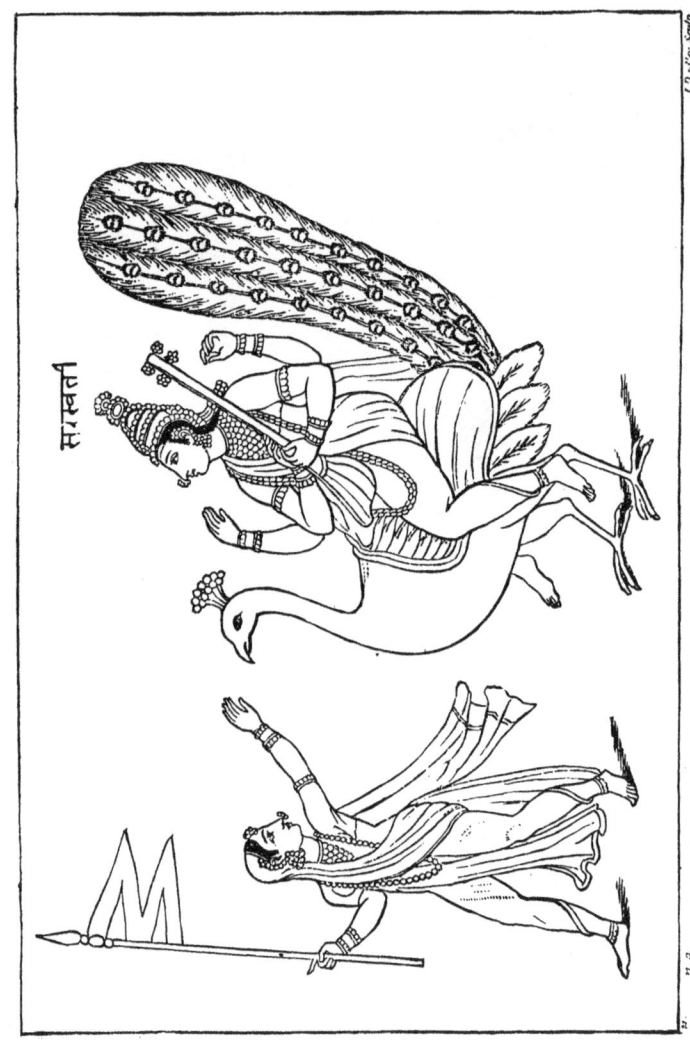

SAR-ISWATI, CONSORT OF BRAHMA, WITH HER PEACOCK AND ATTENDANT.

APPENDIX.

To many persons, doubtless, the foregoing statements of Messrs. Wake and Westropp appear to be grossly exaggerated if not absolutely preposterous. It seems to them almost incredible that such ideas and customs should obtain ascendancy among any people, and especially in the character of religious mysteries. Even classical readers participate in this skepticism. They are unwilling to believe that, except in places notoriously immoral, like Pompeii or Lampsacus, the use of sexual representations in common life would be countenanced. Nevertheless, a careful review of the evidence will assure us of their mistake. We must not always expect shameless manners to attend immorality. Prudery and pruriency are frequently companions, equally impure and cowardly; and in all scientific investigation they should be disregarded rather than conciliated.

The careful student of the Old Testament is amazed at the antagonism apparent between the examples of the Hebrew patriarchs and the teachings of the prophets, in regard to the erection of monolithic pillars and other structures, for votive memorials and other religious purposes. It is likewise hard to distinguish a difference between the customs of the early Israelites and those of the nations around them. The similarity is observable in their religious as well as their political institutions. Their rulers were at first patriarchs or sheiks, as among the Arabs; then they had princes of tribes, like the lords of the Philistines, and after that *suffetes*, or judges, like the Carthaginians; concluding finally with kings, "like all the nations." They had the same language and alphabet as the Phœnicians from the days of Moses. As, despite the tenth chapter of Genesis, the ethnographers persist in classing the latter in the Semitic group, there is little reason given for not including both peoples under one ethnic head.

The Phœnicians and Pelasgians or Ionians of Asia Minor were the most adventurous nations of the time. They colonized Greece, Italy, Spain, and Africa, and the former extended their enterprises to the countries on the Atlantic Ocean. Their gods Baal or Hercules, and Astarté or Venus, were worshipped wherever they went. So uniform were the religious emblems and customs, that a description of the usages of one people very nearly describes them all. The Pelasgians of Ionia had different deity-names, like Dionysus or Bacchus, Hermes, Aphrodité; but they had like customs, and the Cabeirian Mysteries, which fixed the institutions of religion, were common to both.

The Hermaic statue, consisting of a human head placed upon an inverted obelisk, with a phallus, was the recognized simulacrum of Baal in the Bible. Associated with it was the Venus or Aphrodité, a female draped figure terminating below in the same square form. This was generally of wood, the palm being preferred. The name Aspasia is often inscribed upon these female images. The Hermaic and Aphroditic statue were sometimes included in one, like the Hindoo Siva and Bhavani, giving rise to the androgynous representations.

The mode of constructing the Hermaic statues was derived by the Greeks from the Pelasgians of Asia Minor. Herodotus says: " Whoever has been initiated into the Mysteries of the Cabeiri will understand what I mean. The Samothracians received these Mysteries from the Pelasgi, who, before they went to live in Attica, were dwellers in Samothrace, and imparted their religious ceremonies to the inhabitants. The Athenians, then, who were the first of all the Greeks to make their statues of Mercury in this way, learnt the practice from the Pelasgians; and by this people a religious account of the matter is given, which is explained in the Samothracian Mysteries."*

The Cabeiri, we presume, represented the divinities of the planets; Esmun or the Phœnician Esculapius being the eighth. The serpent was his symbol. Kadmiel or Cadmus was the same as Taut or Thoth, the god of the steles or pillar-emblems, and was the reputed founder of the city of Thebes. It was to the worship of these divinities that reference was made by the author of *The Wisdom of Solomon:* " They slew their children in sacrifices, or used secret Mysteries, or celebrated frantic komuses of strange rites." †

But the institution of the Orphic rites and the Eleusinian Mysteries is ascribed by Herodotus to Egyptian influences. "The rites called Orphic and Bacchic are in reality Egyptian and Pythagorean; and no one initiated in these Mysteries can be buried in a woollen shroud, a religious reason being assigned for the observance."‡ Melampus introduced into Greece the name of Dionysus or Bacchus, the ceremonial of his worship, and the procession of the phallus. " I can by no means admit," says Herodotus, "that it is by mere coincidence that the Bacchic ceremonies in Greece are so nearly the same as the Egyptian—they would have been more Greek in their character and less recent in their origin. Much less can I admit that the Egyptians borrowed these customs, or any other, from the Greeks. My belief is that Melampus got his knowledge of them from Cadmus the Tyrian, and the followers whom he brought from Phœnicia into the country which is now called Bœotia." " The Egyptians were also the first to introduce solemn assemblies, processions, and litanies to the gods; of all which the Greeks

---

* Rawlinson's *Herodotus*, book ii. 51. " The phallus formed an essential part of the symbol, probably because the divinity represented by it was in the earliest times, before the worship of Dionysus was imported from the East, the personification of the reproductive powers of nature."—*Smith's Dictionary of Greek and Roman Antiquities, Hermai.*

† *Wisdom*, xiv. 23.

‡ Book ii. 81.

were taught the use by them." * In the Dionysiac festival of Egypt, instead of phalli they used images a cubit high, pulled by strings, which the women carried round to the villages. A piper headed the company, and the women followed, singing hymns in honor of the god. As in the Cabeirian Mysteries of Phœnicia and Samothrace, a "religious reason" accounted for the peculiarities of the image. The identity of Bacchus with the Moloch or Hercules of the Phœnicians, and with the Dionysus of Arabia and the Mysteries, is apparent.

Both the Greeks and Romans, however, for a long time had no images. Numa, who is said to have been a Pythagorean, allowed only the "eternal fire" of Vesta as a symbol of the Deity. The earlier temples were *temenoi*, or consecrated areas, marked out by erect pillars of stone. In them were altars, "great stones," or conical statues. Mounds, or artificial eminences, were also common, as representative of the "holy hill," or mount of assembly where the Deity dwelt. These were denominated, by both Greeks and Phœnicians, *bemas*, or "high places."†

The stele or pillar came early to be used as the emblem of the god; and, in like manner, a conical stone, signifying the omphalos, navel, or rounded abdomen, became the symbol of the great Mother-Goddess. The service of Hercules, with Omphalé, queen or goddess of Lydia, he receiving from her the distaff, and she taking his club and lion-skin, expresses the association of the two in the Mysteries. At the temple of Amun, in Libya, the emblem of the god is described as an *umbriculum* of immense size, which was borne in a boat or ark, requiring eighty men for the purpose.‡ The boat is a feminine symbol. At the temple of Delphi, the omphalos, or navel-stone, is described as obtuse in form, and having nothing obscene in appearance. It was of white marble, and was kept in the sanctuary, carefully wrapped in a white cloth.§ The *nabhi*,

---

* Book ii. 49, 58. ‡ Quintus Curtius.
† Ezekiel xx. 29. § Strabo, book ix. 420.

or navel of Vishnu, the Brahmin god, explained in like manner as expressive of the female organs, is similarly represented. M. Creuzer found among the ruins of Carthage a large conical stone, which he immediately recognized as the representation of Astarté. Lajard also mentions many smaller cones in Greece, some of them bearing the name of Aphrodité. "In all Cyprian coins," he remarks, " may be seen, in the place where we would anticipate to find a statue of the goddess, the form of a conical stone. The same is found placed between two cypresses under the portico of the temple of Astarté, in a temple of Ælia Capitolina; but in this instance the cone is crowned. In another medal, struck by the elder Philip, Venus is represented between two genii, each of whom stands upon a cone or pillar with a rounded top. There is reason to believe that at Paphos images of the conical stone * were made and sold as largely as were effigies of Diana of the Ephesians." † ‡

The ancient Arabians, in like manner, venerated certain conical stones as symbols of the goddess Al Uza, or Alitta. The famous Caaba, or black stone of Mecca, now revered by the Moslems, was of this character. The crescent, also the emblem of the goddess, is the Mohammedan monogram, contrasting with the cross, or masculine emblem of the Christians, and almost implies that the Mussulmans are votaries of the female divinity. The Scandinavians also represented the goddess Disa or Isa by a conical stone, surmounted by a head, analogous to the busts of Astarté.

The erect pillar was common over all the East. It stood at the intersection of roads as a sign of consecra-

---

* "The statue of the goddess bears no resemblance to the human form. It is round throughout, broad at one end, and gradually tapering to a narrow span at the other, like a goal. The reason is stated by Philostratus to be symbolical."—*Tacitus*, book ii., ch. 3.

† Acts xix. 24, 25. Venus and Diana, instead of representing the opposing ideas of virginity and sexual love, were deities of like mould, and personified the great maternal principle.

‡ *Recherches sur la Culte de Vénus*, page 36.

tion, on the boundaries of estates, in and before temples, over graves, and wherever the deities were venerated. At Athens was a "pillar of the Amazon" or androgynous Venus; and Apollonius mentions a *lithos hieros* or sacred stone in the temple of Arez in Pontus, where the Amazons worshipped. Like columns were common in Thessaly, Ionia, and Mauritania; and, indeed, in all countries washed by the sea. The Round Towers of Ireland, the great stones found in the principal point of cities in England, the stones of memorial in all parts of the British Isles, including "Jacob's pillar" transported from Scotland by Edward I., and now preserved in the seat of the Coronation Chair in Westminster Abbey, pertain to the same cultus. The Maypoles, common alike to Britons and Hindus, are of one pattern. The Buddhists of Ceylon, the Sivaists and Lingayats of Hindustan, and the Zoroastrians of Persia, have these emblems like their fellow-religionists of the West.

Nor was ancient America any exception to these customs. A plain cylindrical stone was to be found by every Mexican temple. At Copan are monoliths, some of them in a rough state and others sculptured. At Honduras is an "idol of round stone" with two faces, representing the Lord of Life, which the Indians adore, offering blood procured from the prepuce. In Panuco was found in the temples a phallus, and on bas-reliefs in public places were depicted the sacred *membra conjuncta in coitu*. There were also similar symbols in Tlascala. On one of the phallic pillars at Copan were also the emblems relative to uterine existence, parturition, etc. Juan de Batanzos, in his *History of the Incas*, an unpublished manuscript in the Library of the Escurial, says that "in the centre of the great square or court of the Temple of the Sun at Cuzco, was a column or pillar of stone, of the shape of a loaf of sugar, pointed at the top and covered with gold-leaf." *

It is probable that the mound-builders of North America were votaries of the same worship. Professor Troost has

* Squier's *Serpent Symbol*, p. 50.

procured several images in Smith county, Tennessee, one of which was endowed disproportionately, like a Pan or Hermes, or the idol at Lampsacus. The phallus had been broken off, while in the ground, by a plough. Dr. Ramsay, of Knoxville, also describes two phallic similacra in his possession, twelve and fifteen inches in length. The shorter one was of amphibolic rock, and so very hard that steel could make no impression upon it. The Abbé de Bourbourg, who made careful explorations in Mexico and Central America, confirms the statements in regard to the phallic symbolism, and apparently supposes that it was introduced from America into Europe.

The Cross was also found among the ruins of the American temples. In Mexico it was the Egyptian symbol, the *crux ansata*, and was denominated " the tree of life." Its frequency over the Eastern continent, pertaining alike to the worship of Osiris, Baal-Adonis, Mithra, and Mahadeva, is well known. The Buddhists of Tibet employ it in worship, and place it, like the Hermaic pillars, at the corners of the street. It was sculptured beside the lingam or phallus, in the cave of Elephanta. The Hindoo cross resembles the " hammer of Thor." In the tombs of Etruria were found crosses composed of four phalli. Similar to this was the cross of Malta, till it was changed to its present shape.

The use of votive amulets in that phallic form was also common. They were found in the tombs and houses. Similar articles are now manufactured in India. The Hindoo women carry the lingam in procession between two serpents; and it will be remembered that in the sacred ark or coffer which held the egg and phallus in the mystic processions of the Greeks, was also a serpent. In Greece and Western Asia the favorite wood for the " stocks" and phallic pillars, according to St. Clement of Alexandria, was the fig. The leaves of this tree, it will be remembered, were used in the garden of Eden; and the fruit has had a peculiar symbolical meaning for thousands of years.

That the ancient patriarchs, like the patriarchs and chiefs of other nations, erected pillars and altars, and worshipped in mountains and high places, is matter of record. The pillars at Bethel and Mizpeh, set up by Jacob, were revered by his descendants. Mizpeh was a holy place, during the days of the Judges; Jephthah made it his seat of government, and after him Samuel was inaugurated there. The Israelites met there to put away Baalim and Ashtaroth, as enjoined by the prophet; who, after that, made a yearly circuit to Bethel, Gilgal, and Mizpeh, and had his residence at Ramah, where was a "high place."

The dances, or *komuses*, were also celebrated, as in the festivals of Bacchus.* King David himself, in his joy at the bringing of the ark to Jerusalem, "danced before the Lord," and being rebuked by his wife, Michal, for his wanton deportment, declared that was in the presence of Jehovah, adding that he would "play" and be yet "more vile." Whether phalli were carried by the Hebrew women at their dances and festivals, as among the Greeks and Asiatics, is not stated, but it is not improbable. The prophets denounce the festivals and solemn assemblies as attended with idolatrous and obscene rites.

The worship of the Phœnician deities continued among the Israelites throughout the whole period of the rule of the Judges.† The Philistines also had the same divinities. When the body of King Saul fell into their hands, they dedicated his armor as a trophy in the temple of Astarté; and according to one author, placed his head in the temple of Dagon the Fish-god, and according to another, his body on the wall of the temple of San.‡ After the establishment of the monarchy, the idolatrous rites took a more objectionable form. King Solomon is recorded to have built *mounds* or high places for Chemosh, the god of generation, and for Hercules or Moloch, the god of fire, and to have worshipped Venus-Astarté.

---

* Judges xxi. 19–23.
† Judges ii. 10–19; iii. 6, 7; v. 8; vi. 10, 25, 30; viii. 33; x. 6.
‡ 1 Samuel xxxi. 9, 10, and 1 Chronicles x. 9, 10.

These shrines remained throughout the Hebrew monarchy, till Josiah profaned them, broke down the pillars, and took away the omphalic symbols, filling their places with the bones of men. So general had been the prevalence of idolatry, and especially of the Tyrian worship, that these "high places" existed all over the country, with the phallic statues and omphalic emblems, "on every high hill, and under every green tree." * That they became places of prostitution, if they were not such at the first, seems to be the concurrent testimony of the prophets and profane writers. Whether the sacrifice of virginity was made at these places, as at the temples of Mylitta, and other divinities, is not expressly affirmed; but the presence of the *kadeshim* is suspicious.†

The Hebrew prophets are outspoken in associating Baal-worship with lewdness. Hosea, using the customary parallelism of expression, identifies the priapic cultus with that of Peor. "They went to Baal-Peor, and consecrated

* 1 Kings xiv. 23. See also xv. 14; xxii. 43; 2 Kings xii. 3; xiv. 4; xv. 4 and 35; xvi. 4; xvii. 9, 10.

† See 1 Kings xiv. 23, 24; xv. 12 and xxii. 46; 2 Kings xxxiii. 7; Hosea iv. 10-19 and v. 4. The Kings Asa and Jehoshaphat drove these persons from the country. They appear to have been of foreign blood; the book of Deuteronomy prescribing that they should not be Israelites. "There shall be no *kadeshah* of the daughters of Israel, nor a *kadesh* of the sons of Israel," —xxiii. 17. It is evident, however, that the Israelites imputed no merit, but rather opprobrium, to the virgin state. When Jephthah announced to his daughter that he had made an irrevocable vow to offer her in sacrifice, she only pleaded for a respite of two months to "go up and down upon the mountains, and bewail her virginity." This is apparently in accord with the statement of Mindes-Pinto, that the young Indian maids believe it impossible for a virgin to enter Paradise. The readiness of the Israelites to adopt the rites of Venus and Baal-Peor (Exodus xxxii. 6, 25, and Numbers xxv.) would seem to be thus explained. The worship of the goddess Diana or Venus-Anaitis in Armenia was attended by the defloration of nubile women. The Babylonian colonists of Samaria brought with them the worship of the Succoth-Benoth, or the Venuses of the tents; and it is certain that *almas* or consecrated women, as in Egypt, and nautch-girls or women of the temple, were a peculiarity of Phœnician, as they are of Hindoo sanctuaries. Justin relates that Dido or Elissa transported twenty-four of these females to Carthage. The name Elissa or Alitta being a title of the goddess, shows that her expedition is but an allegory to explain the introduction of her worship into the countries

themselves to *Bosheth*." * Jeremiah also is unmistakable. "According to the number of thy cities were thy gods, Oh Judah! and according to the number of the streets of Jerusalem [as in Tyre and Athens] have ye set up altars to *Bosheth*, even altars to burn incense to Baal." † These were "the iniquities of their forefathers."

The worship of the Queen of Heaven, Mylitta or the Syrian goddess, "the children gathering wood, the fathers kindling the fire, and the women kneading the dough to make cakes," is instanced several times by Jeremiah; and was an old custom, observed alike by kings, nobles, and the common people.‡ The cake was made of flour and honey, and was shaped like a lozenge or phallus. The *cunim* or *bouns* were offered to Astarté and Aphrodité wherever they were worshipped, at the opening of spring.

The sacrifice of children, common among the Phœnicians and their colonies, was also a practice of the Jews. Sometimes it was only a passing through the fire, as at the Bal-tines of Scotland and Ireland; at others, it was

---

of the West. The island of Melita was named from this divinity. Ovid describes her festival:

> " On the Ides is the genial feast of Anna perenna,
> Not far, traveller Tiber, from thy banks.
> The people come, and scattered everywhere among the green stalks,
> Imbibe, and each reclines with his female consort.
> Part remain in the open air, a few set up tents;
> Some out of branches have made a leafy hut."—*Fasti*, iv.

The Indian Anna-purna, and the Babylonian Daughter of the Tent, are easily recognized. In Virgil's Æneid, Anna is made the sister of Elissa.

* Hosea ix. 10. The "high place" of Baal where Balak and Balaam met to invoke curses upon Israel (Numbers xxii. 41). The term בשת, *bosheth*, here used as the synonyme for Baal, signifies the *phallus*. It is also translated *shame*—Jeremiah iii. 24, and Micah i. 11—but doubtless means Baal-worship in both instances. The two words were compounded interchangeably in proper names. Jerub-baal or Gideon was also styled Jerub-besheth; Ish-Bosheth, the son of Saul, and Mephi-Bosheth, the son of Jonathan, were transcribed by the synonymes Esh-Baal and Merib-Baal in the first Book of Chronicles.

† Jeremiah xi. 13.

‡ Jeremiah vii. 17–31 and xliv. 8, 15–23.

Appendix. 89

"the shedding of innocent blood." * The sacrifices were made to the fire-god Moloch, or Baal-Hercules. In Isaiah, however, we find mention made of "slaying the children in the valleys under the clefts of the rocks."† This must have been an offering to Astarté. These were the *cunni diaboli*, or emblems of maternity, closely related to the omphalic stones. The one at Delphi emitted a gas which the priestess inhaled before delivering her oracles. They are abundant in India at the present day, and were formerly in England before the introduction of Christianity. Miss Ellwood, in her *Journey to the East*, mentions one which she saw: "There is a sacred perforated stone at Malabar, through which penitents squeezed themselves in order to obtain a remission of their sins.‡

The custom of burning the thigh in sacrifices, which was universal, is of the same character. The golden thigh of Pythagoras was doubtless the thing last revealed to the initiate. It was the *meros* in which the fœtal Bacchus was preserved; and, like the phallus shown to the epopt at Eleusis, prefigured the great mystery of life.

It is noticeable that all these sensual peculiarities pertained to the worship of the female divinities. The priests of Hercules, as of the *lingam* in India, were monks. The Hellenic Jew explains it like the more orthodox prophets, that "the devising of images was the beginning of lewdness, and the invention of them the corruption of life." §

Nevertheless we also are not prepared to accept unqualifiedly the sentiment that "Human nature is the same in all climes, and the workings of this same human nature are almost identical in their different stages of growth." If Mr. Westropp means from this that we should infer that the employment of the sexual symbolism in worship is characteristic of all mankind at a peculiar stage of devel-

* 2 Kings xvi. 3; xxi. 6, 16 and xxiv. 4; 2 Chronicles xxviii. 3; Jeremiah ii. 34, 35 and xix. 4; Psalm cvi. 34–39.
† Isaiah lvii. 5.
‡ *Our British Ancestors*, p. 160.
§ *Wisdom of Solomon*, xiv. 12.

opment, we dissent. Besides, there are tribes that we must acknowledge as human beings, having no customs entitled to be regarded as a cultus. Races of men are materially diverse in structure, type, and psychical character, and probably had their origins in climates and periods of time widely apart from each other. "Human nature is manifestly very unlike, as exhibited respectively by the European populations, the Chinese, the African negroes, and the Australians."

Our evidence as to the antiquity of this peculiar symbolism is necessarily very incomplete. There have been endeavors to solve the question by an ingenious calculation. The Maypole festival, common to all ancient countries east and west, and well known to have a phallic origin, should be dated from the vernal equinox, when that was the period of the entering of the sun into the zodiacal sign Taurus. Counting seventy-two years for the precession of the sun a single degree, the precise period of that occurrence was about four thousand years before the Christian era.* The Maypole celebration, if we adopt the popular chronology, must have therefore taken its inception from some event connected with the occurrences recorded as happening in the Garden of Eden.†

The principal Aryan nations appear to have displayed a determined hostility to the entire phallic symbolism. In the Rig-Veda, the *sisna-devas* or priests of the lingam are debarred from access to the sacred rites,‡ and con-

---

* *The Round Towers of Ireland*, pp. 233, 234; also Maurice's *Indian Antiquities*.

† Nevertheless, there may be reason, instead, to assign a date some time in the pre-Adamite period. In the *Moniteur* of January, 1865, it is stated that in the province of Venetia, in Italy, excavations in a bone-cave brought to light, beneath ten feet of stalagmite, bones of animals, mostly post-tertiary, of the usual description found in such places, flint implements, with a needle of bone having an eye and point, and a plate of an argillaceous compound, on which was scratched a rude drawing of a phallus.

‡ A similar prohibition appears also in the last stages of the Hebrew monarchy. When Josiah abolished the worship at the "high places," he refused to admit the priests that had officiated at them, to the service of the Temple. The prophet Ezekiel also promulgated the following ordinance against them:

signed to destruction at the hands of Indra. The invaders of India could find no milder language for the lascivious religionists whom they encountered than demons, devil-worshippers, and persons who observe no sacred rites. The Brahmin system was adopted afterward, unwillingly, as a compromise.

The ancient Persians exhibited a like detestation of the icon-worshippers. "They had no images of the gods, no temples, nor altars, and considered the use of them a sign of folly."* The Achæmenian kings were worshippers of Ormazd, and displayed a similar antagonism to that of their Vedic brethren to the current idolatrous practices of their time. Eventually the magian system of Media and Babylonia was engrafted upon the popular worship of Persia, although the kings and nobler classes adhered to the Zoroastrian doctrines.

These doctrines appear to be so closely allied to those imputed to Moses, that it is not difficult to imagine that they had once been identical. The exiles who returned from beyond the Euphrates are described very differently from those who were transported by Nebuchadnezzar.†

"They shall not come near unto me to do the office of a priest unto me, nor come near to any of my holy things in the most holy place; but they shall bear their shame, and their abominations which they have committed." xliv. 6-14.

* Herodotus, i. 131.

† The colonization of the Jews in Palestine under Cyrus and his successors appears very like a new occupation, rather than a return. It is evident that there were more of them beyond the Euphrates than ever made their homes in Judea. Their leading class bore the title of Pharisees, perhaps from their Persian affiliations. They, according to Spinoza, made the selection of the books which are now accepted as the Sacred Scriptures, adopting only those which had been composed in the Hebrew language. The text of this was revised and pruned, and occasionally changed. It seems to have been their purpose to keep the knowledge of it in the limits of their own order. Nevertheless, it betrays the indications of an Ionian influence, and also of a Hindoo antecedent. The patriarchal names are very similar to those of the Brahmin divinities: Brahma and his consort Sara-Iswati, his son Ikshwaka, and great-grandson Yadu. The ruins of the temple of Peace, or Tukht Solumi, have been found in Cashmere, and many names of the Bible and Western Asia, like Yudia, Dawid, Arabi, Cush, Yavan, are also indigenous to the region of the Indus.

They no more filled their land with idolatry and phallic emblems, but simply placed the sacred fire in the temple at Jerusalem and watched against its extinction. The precept of the law of Moses forbidding the fabricating and adoration of *pesels* or graven images, was rigidly kept. Synagogues for religious instruction took the place of high places, pillars, and enclosures of a circular form. Whatever may have been the characteristics of their ancestors before the captivity, they were true afterward to the lessons learned in exile. In the reign of Antiochus they resisted the introduction of the mysteries of Dionysus, and underwent tortures and crucifixion rather than taste the flesh of swine and participate in the foreign worship.

The transition from the old Roman and ethnic religions to Christianity could not possibly be effected so completely as to change entirely the real sentiments of the people. We must not be surprised, therefore, when we are told that the ancient worship, after it had been excluded from its former temples and from the metropolitan towns, was maintained for a long time by the inhabitants of humbler localities. Indeed, from this very fact it obtained its subsequent designation. From being kept up in the villages (or *pagi*), its votaries were denominated pagans, *pagani*, or villagers.

The prevalence of Mithraic or magian ideas and practices led also to the confounding of the proscribed worship with the practice of witchcraft and sorcery; and to this fact we are indebted for the numerous legends and accounts of secret colleges of magicians, as well as of assemblies of witches in remote places, decorated with the symbols of the old religion, of kings or devils having the goat-form of the ancient Pan or Bacchus with the priapic appendages, of distinguished persons in attendance in the habit of satyrs, of sham sacraments like those of the Persian god Mithras, and especially of the orgies or enthusiastic furors, together with general debauchery. There is little reason to doubt that these "witches' sabbaths" were formerly celebrated, and that they were, in some modified form, a continuation of the outlawed worship of the Roman Empire.*

Whether the alarm experienced in this country two centuries ago, of an invasion of Satan and his associated powers, was a delusion,† or had some relation to the possible introduction of the old Asiatic and Roman religion into America, is a question admitting of ingenious discussion. In Europe, however, its maintenance, after many centuries had elapsed of proscription and persecution, finally became impossible. The ignorance of the common people rendered them ill-adapted to continue a worship so full of recondite mystery, and the orgies or "sabbaths" fell into neglect. But in certain practices and superstitions not yet outgrown, the old phallism and pagan ideas still crop out. Good and ill fortune are supposed to result from the wholesome or obnoxious influence of the moon. Goethe has commemorated the potency of the pentacle as a protector against evil spirits. The mystic horse-shoe, a uterine symbol, is still employed.‡ Lucky and unlucky days are regarded. Even at the gaming-table, the cards are indicated by the phallic symbols, the spade and triadic club, and the omphalic distaff and eminence disguised as the heart and diamond. Certain peculiarities of architecture and decoration are inspired from the same source, and whoever is intelligent is not slow to recognize the fact.

* The heretical sects, as they sprung up, were denounced in the same manner. Even to this day, *Vauderie*, or Vaudois worship, is the French designation for witchcraft; and the name of Bulgarians [*Bulgres*], who were once Albigenses or Paulicians, is now applied to men practising unnatural vice.

† The apprehension of this invasion was entertained in all the British North American Colonies, and the severest penal laws were enacted in consequence. The executions in Massachusetts, in 1692, operated to overthrow the prevailing sentiment in that region; but in New York and the other provinces, the laws were enforced till the Revolution. Indeed, in South Carolina witchcraft was a capital offence in the Code till the reorganization of the State government after the recent civil war; and less than a century ago offenders were executed.

‡ In a church in Paris is said to be a relic of special virtue, the *pudenda muliebria Sanctæ Virginis*. See Inman's *Ancient Faiths Embodied in Ancient Names*, vol. i., p. 144.

In popular customs, and even in religious institutions, these things are as plainly to be perceived to-day as when Adonis and Astarté were the gods of the former world. The sanctities, the powers, the symbols, and even the utensils of the ancient Faith, have been assumed, if not usurped or legitimately inherited, by its successors. The two holies of the Gnostics and Neo-Platonists, Sophia and Eirené, wisdom and peace, were adopted as saints into the calendar of Constantinople. Dionysus, the god of the Mysteries, reappears as St. Denys in France, St. Liberius, St. Eleutherius, and St. Bacchus; there is also a St. Mithra; and even Satan, prince of shadows, is revered as St. Satur and St. Swithin. Their relics are in keeping. The Holy Virgin Astræa or Astarté, whose return was announced by Virgil in the days of Augustus, as introducing a new Golden Age, now under her old designation of Blessed Virgin and Queen of Heaven, receives homage as "the one whose sole divinity the whole orb of the earth venerates." The Mother and Child, the latter adorned with the nimbus or aureole of the ancient sun-gods, are now the object of veneration as much as were Ceres and Bacchus, or Isis and Horus in the Mysteries. Nuns abound alike in Christian and in Buddhist countries, as they did formerly in Isis-worshipping Egypt; and if their maidenhood is not sacrificed at the shrine of Baal-Peor, or any of his cognate divinities, yet it is done in a figure: they are all "brides of the Saviour." *Galli* sing in the churches, and consecrated women are as numerous as of old. The priestly vestments are like those formerly used in the worship of Saturn and Cybelé; the Phrygian cap, the pallium, the stole, and the alb. The whole pantheon has been exhausted from the Indus, Euphrates, and the Nile, to supply symbolic adornment for the apostles' successors. Hercules holds the distaff of Omphalé. The Lily has superseded the Lotus, and celibacy is exalted above the first recorded mandate of God to mankind.

In ancient times the Carians and other votaries used to wound themselves and offer their blood to Bacchus in commemoration of his dismemberment by the Titans. The former worshippers in Yucatan and Central America had an analogous custom. The prophets of Baal in Syria and Phœnicia also inflicted wounds on themselves.* The Jews were prohibited from this by their law,† but at the period of mourning for the dead one, Adonis, slain by the boar, they flogged themselves and wept. This animal, which was sacred to Mars or Ares, the god of destruction, became their abomination. The Egyptians had a like custom. At the assemblies of Isis, composed of many thousands of pilgrims, those who participated in the solemnities scourged themselves in memory of the slaughtered Oseiris.‡ Sailors were whipped around the altar of Apollo at Delos, and children at the temple of Diana in Sparta. In Rome, at the Lupercalia, about the 14th of February, young men used to lay aside their garments, and taking whips, run through the streets, flogging everybody whom they met.§ Even now, during Holy Week in Rome, many devotees lash themselves till the blood gushes in streams; and the same practice exists in other places. The Flagellants of the Middle Ages appear to have been actuated by a similar enthusiasm.

The pretension to universal supremacy by leading Bishops of the earlier centuries is familiar to all who are conversant with church history. The Grand Lama of the Buddhists, and the *Zeus* or *Archiereus* of old Hellas, furnished antetypes which were speedily imitated at the

* 1 Kings xviii. 28.
† Leviticus xix. 28 and xxi. 5.
‡ Herodotus, ii. 61.
§ There seems to be a voluptuous sense excited in this way. Women, especially those who were married, eagerly placed themselves in the way of these flagellators, partly on account of the exquisite delight received from the infliction, and partly because of the idea that it promoted the aptitude to conceive. The late Henry Buckle, author of the *History of Civilization*, printed privately a series of curious tracts on this subject, illustrating how a practice beginning in religious zeal can be made a source of sensuous delight.— *Rare Tracts on Flagellation*. Reprinted from the original editions collected by the late Henry Thomas Buckle. 7 vols. post 8vo. London. Printed by G. Peacock, 1777.

focal points of the Empire. The Bishop of Rome, however, was the most successful. In his person the *Pontifex Maximus* exists as in the days of the Republic and the Cæsars. Asia and Italy alike minister to his elevation. He has "the power of the keys," the key of Janus of archaic Rome, and the key of Cybelé, the Virgin-Mother of Asia. The former was *patulcius* and *clusius*, the opener and shutter; and with the authority of Cybelé he was empowered also, as the *vesica piscis* indicates, to superintend the gateway of physical existence. But let there be no sneer at this. In the Catacombs of Rome, where the early Christians used to congregate, are numerous pictures and carvings indicating close resemblances to the pagan usages. Enough exists to show that the pontiff does not take all by assumption. The utensils and other furniture of the Mysteries appear to have been there; and one drawing shows a woman standing before an altar offering bunns to the Serpent-divinity. It is true, doubtless, that there is not a fast or festival, procession or sacrament, social custom or religious symbol, that did not come "bodily" from the previous paganism. But the Pope did not import them on his own account; they had already been transferred into the ecclesiastical structure, and he only accepted and perhaps took advantage of the fact. Many of those who protest because of these "corruptions," are prone to imitate them, more or less, displaying an engrafting from the same stock.

Much dispute has been had in regard to the presence of St. Peter at Rome. The statue of the apostle, it has been asserted with great plausibility, was originally the bust of the Jupiter of the Capitol. We presume that the "apostle of the circumcision," as Paul, his great rival, styles him, was never at the Imperial City, nor had a successor there, not even in the Ghetto. The "Chair of Peter,"* therefore,

---

* There appear to have been two chairs of the titular apostle. In the year 1662 the workmen engaged in cleaning one of them for exhibition to the people, on the 18th of January, "the Twelve Labors of Hercules unluckily appeared

is sacred rather than apostolical. Its sanctity proceeded, however, from the esoteric religion of the former times of Rome. The hierophant of the Mysteries probably occupied it on the day of initiations, when exhibiting to the candidates the *petroma*.*

The end crowned the work. "In the Church of St. Peter's at Rome," Godfrey Higgins asserts, † "is kept *in secret* a large stone emblem of the creative power, of a very peculiar shape, on which are the words, Ζευς Σωτηρ, Zeus Soter (or Jove the Saviour); only persons who have great interest can get a sight of it."

Thus the cycle seems to return upon itself. Archaic Rome seems to live again in the Rome Mediæval, old Egypt and Babylonia to be resuscitated in our modern Europe. Yet this is not altogether true. Let us take heed how we hear.

Those capable of understanding, will recognize in this symbolism the revelation of the first creation and the re-

engraved on it." (Bower's *History of the Popes*, vol. ii., p. 7.) This chair was removed and another substituted. In 1795 the French under Bonaparte occupied Rome, and again the chair was investigated. This time there was found the Mohammedan Confession of Faith, in Arabic letters: "There is no deity but Allah, and Mohammed is his Apostle." Zodiacs, or Labors of Hercules, evidently of an astrological character, have been found in the churches of York and Lyons, and a wine-cask at the shrine of St. Denys. On the hypothesis of having been heir-looms from the pagan religion, these facts are duly accounted for, except the French discovery. It may have been that Islam and the Papacy once contemplated an alliance, or some crusader brought the chair from the East.

* If this supposition is correct, the ecclesiastical legends of Peter's sojourn at Rome are easily comprehended. The *petroma*, or stone tablet, contained or constituted the last revelation made by the hierophant to the candidate for initiation. What it was might never be divulged on pain of death. All the work of the Creator was now unfolded, and the profane might not know the solemn secret. As the Mysteries came to Rome from the East, it is easy to perceive that the hierophant or revelator would have an oriental title. *Peter*, from the Phœnician word פתר, *peter*, is applied in the Book of Genesis (xl. 8) to an expounder of dreams, and was probably the designation of the interpreter of the *petroma*. The Roman Bishop succeeding to his chair, would be, it is apparent, pontiff over the whole world.

† *Celtic Druids*, pp. 195-196.

naissance, as refined in sentiment or as gross in sense as is the mind of the person witnessing the vision. Whether he has learned supernal mysteries is to be ascertained ; certainly he is revealed to himself, humbled if not humble.

OTHER TITLES AVAILABLE THROUGH THE BOOK TREE • CALL FOR OUR FREE CATALOG

TRIUMPH OF THE HUMAN SPIRIT: *The Greatest Achievements of the Human Soul and How Its Power Can Change Your Life* by Paul Tice. A triumph of the human spirit happens when we know we are right about something, put our heart into achieving its goal, and then succeed. There is no better feeling. People throughout history have triumphed while fighting for the highest ideal of all – spiritual truth. Some of these people and movements failed, other times they changed the course of history. Those who failed only did so on a physical level, when they were eliminated through violence. Their spirit lives on. This book not only documents the history of spiritual giants, it shows you how you can achieve your own spiritual triumph. Various exercises will strengthen your soul and reveal its hidden power. In today's world we are free to explore the truth without fear of being tortured or executed. As a result, the rewards are great. You will discover your true spiritual power with this work and will be able to tap into it. This is the perfect book for all those who believe in spiritual freedom and have a passion for the truth. **(1999) • 295 pages • 6 x 9 • trade paperback • $19.95 • ISBN 1-885395-57-4**

PAST SHOCK: *The Origin of Religion and Its Impact on the Human Soul* by Jack Barranger. Introduction by Paul Tice. Twenty years ago, Alvin Toffler coined the term "future shock" – a syndrome in which people are overwhelmed by the future. *Past Shock* suggests that events which happened thousands of years ago very strongly impact humanity today. This book reveals incredible observations on our inherited "slave chip" programming and how w've been conditioned to remain spiritually ignorant. Barranger exposes what he calls the "pretender gods," advanced beings who were not divine, but had advanced knowledge of scientific principles which included genetic engineering. Our advanced science of today has unraveled their secrets, and people like Barranger have the knowledge and courage to expose exactly how we were manipulated. Readers will learn about our past conditioning, and how to overcome the "slave chip" mentality to begin living life as it was meant to be, as a spiritually fulfilled being. **(1998) • 126 pages • 6 x 9 • trade paperback • $12.95 • ISBN 1-885395-08-6**

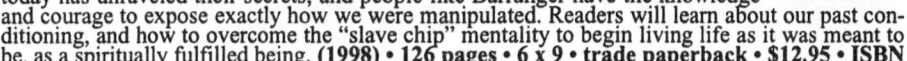

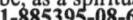

GOD GAMES: *What Do You Do Forever?* by Neil Freer. Introduction by Zecharia Sitchin. This new book by the author of Breaking the Godspell clearly outlines the entire human evolutionary scenario. While Sitchin has delineated what happened to humankind in the remote past based on ancient texts, Freer outlines the implications for the future. We are all creating the next step we need to take as we evolve from a genetically engineered species into something far beyond what we could ever imagine. We can now play our own "god games." We are convinced that great thinkers in the future will look back on this book, in particular, as being the one which opened the door to a new paradigm now developing. Neil Freer is a brilliant philosopher who recognizes the complete picture today, and is far ahead of all others who wonder what really makes us tick, and where it is that we are going. This book will make readers think in new and different ways. **(1998) • 310 pages • 6 x 9 • trade paperback • $19.95 • ISBN 1-885395-26-4**

OF HEAVEN AND EARTH: *Essays Presented at the First Sitchin Studies Day.* Edited by Zecharia Sitchin. Zecharia Sitchin's previous books have sold millions around the world. This book contains further information on his incredible theories about the origins of mankind and the intervention by intelligences beyond the Earth. This book offers the complete proceedings of the first Sitchin Studies Day. Sitchin's keynote address opens the book, followed by six other prominent speakers whose work has been influenced by Sitchin. The other contributors include two university professors, a clergyman, a UFO expert, a philosopher, and a novelist – who joined Zecharia Sitchin to describe how his findings and conclusions have affected what they teach and preach. They all seem to agree that the myths of ancient peoples were actual events as opposed to being figments of imaginations. Another point of agreement is in Sitchin's work being the early part of a new paradigm – one that is already beginning to shake the very foundations of religion, archaeology and our society in general. **(1996) • 164 pages • 5 1/2 x 8 1/2 • trade paperback • $14.95 • ISBN 1-885395-17-5**

FLYING SERPENTS AND DRAGONS: *The Story of Mankind's Reptilian Past*, By R.A. Boulay. Revised and expanded edition. This highly original work deals a shattering blow to all our preconceived notions about our past and human origins. Worldwide legends refer to giant flying lizards and dragons which came to this planet and founded the ancient civilizations of Mesopotamia, Egypt, India and China. Who were these reptilian creatures? This book provides the answers to many of the riddles of history such as what was the real reason for man's creation, why did Adam lose his chance at immortality in the Garden of Eden, who were the Nefilim who descended from heaven and mated with human women, why the serpent take such a bum rap in history, why didn't Adam and Eve wear clothes in Eden, what were the "crystals" or "stones" that the ancient gods fought over, why did the ancient Sumerians call their major gods USHUMGAL, which means literally "great fiery, flying serpent," what was the role of the gigantic stone platform at Baalbek, and what were the "boats of heaven" in ancient Egypt and the "sky chariots" of the Bible? **(1997, 1999) • 276 pages • 5 1/2 x 8 1/2 • trade paperback • $19.95 • ISBN 1-885395-25-6**

Call for our FREE BOOK TREE CATALOG with over 1100 titles. Order from your local bookstore, or we accept Visa, MC, AmEx, or send check or money order (in USD) for the total amount plus 4.50 shipping for 1-3 books (and .50¢ thereafter). The Book Tree • PO Box 724 • Escondido, CA 92033 • (760) 489-5079 • Visit www.thebooktree.com • Call today (800) 700-TREE

www.ingramcontent.com/pod-product-compliance
Lightning Source LLC
Chambersburg PA
CBHW031649040426
42453CB00006B/253

9 781585 090488